Club '43

by
Tina Lesher

Bloomington, IN Milton Keynes, UK

AuthorHouse™
1663 Liberty Drive, Suite 200
Bloomington, IN 47403
www.authorhouse.com
Phone: 1-800-839-8640

AuthorHouse™ UK Ltd.
500 Avebury Boulevard
Central Milton Keynes, MK9 2BE
www.authorhouse.co.uk
Phone: 08001974150

First published by AuthorHouse 6/14/2006

ISBN: 1-4259-4053-6 (sc)

Printed in the United States of America
Bloomington, Indiana

This book is printed on acid-free paper.

Cover Art by Linnea Rhodes

Club'43

Contents

Introduction

These stories amaze me...

That is what I have been uttering to myself for more than two decades, ever since the formation of Club '43, a small---maybe unique---organization of now 60-ish suburban women.

The Club '43 members, including yours truly, wound up living in the same New Jersey town--- Westfield---considered a fairly affluent community 25 miles west of Manhattan. Most arrived courtesy of their spouses' jobs---after all, Westfield is a bedroom community for the New York financial markets and is close to the headquarters of a score of major U. S. firms. The town of 30,000 residents is known for its strong school system, its wealth of stately homes on tree-lined avenues, and its vibrant downtown replete with heralded restaurants and a variety of shopping offerings.

What makes Club '43 unusual stems from the fact that all of us are the same age; we were born in 1943 as the nation was at the height of a great war. Our six decades have taken us through many historical moments. We have been witness to changes that have allowed us to pursue careers and lifestyles that do not mirror those of women a generation ago.

So here we are, a group of 12 Westfielders---all born in 1943--- whose lives are tied to history and to modernity.

Over the years, I listened to these women relate fascinating tales of their lives and varied interests. I became mesmerized by their stories; each woman could relate anecdotal experiences that proved mind-boggling to me.

So, with my journalistic background as a catalyst, I decided to interview and profile these extraordinary women who represent the new sexagenarians (is that an oxymoron?). The result, I hope, extends beyond the basic storytelling of their lives and into the tunnels of history through which they have walked, from World War II to the Internet age of the 21st century.

I hope you enjoy reading about these women.

Tina Rodgers Lesher
Westfield, N.J.
tinalesher@comcast.net

Milestone Celebrations:

The 40th Birthday

It was 1983 and I was heading for my 40th birthday later that year. Westfielder Patty Noerr, whom I knew because our children attended the same local public school, also was turning 40 in '83. Learning about other women also slated to mark their special 40th birthdays the same year, Patty arranged a lunch at a local restaurant to mark the joint occasion. As I recall, five or six were present that day.

One person---I am not sure who---got the idea that we should formalize our birthday relationship and celebrate together in some fun way.

Since we all were born in 1943, we arrived at the group's name: Club '43.

We decided to mark our 40th birthdays in an unusual way. Through word-of-mouth, we would recruit some other women born in 1943 and challenge a group of other Westfield women to a friendly game of softball with a beer bash to follow.

We arrived at Franklin School Field in our "uniforms:" jeans and pink tee shirts emblazoned with a drawing of four women at a spa. No doubt we had made our purchase at a local shirt sale, because most of us had never been to a spa at that point.

Our equipment mirrored a garage sale of sports items: our kids' mitts, some used balls taken from neighbors' basements, and bases "borrowed" without permission from the school where one of our team members taught. Two younger friends, Betty Jordan and Fran Comstock, solicited others to form the opposition team that enjoyed the one-night rivalry. But they did not enjoy the loss---Club '43, with Linnea Rhodes on the mound and Cathy Rock socking hits, overpowered the opponents who had to pay for the beer. It proved to be a fun night.

We did get together a few times during that year, and we kept abreast of each person's birthday by sending cards or going out to lunch.

Club '43 faded into a lack of activity as we moved through our 40s. But the 40th birthday game was the subject of conversation as we crossed each others' paths on the soccer and football fields where our children competed. Our mantra seemed to be: "Get ready for the 50th!"

The 50th Birthday

In January 1993, I joined a few other Club '43 members in setting up a meeting to discuss how we might jointly celebrate our 50th natal days.

It turned out to be quite a year. First, we sent a press release to the local paper; in the article, we asked any woman, who was born in 1943 and who lived or worked in Westfield, to join our unique group.

The result: our membership grew to about 20 members.

Our first objective? To celebrate each member's birthday. Mary Herald, a physician and new member recruited by one of her patients, offered to have her spouse make a sign that we could place on each member's home on the respective date of her birthday.

We expected a sign----a simple sign.

Well, it actually turned out to be two wooden signs, each about four-feet high and two feet wide. One sign said 5 and the other 0. Trekking them from a storage area in a member's garage to a Westfield front lawn took a station wagon, one of those suburban-mother vehicles we all drove prior to the arrival of SUVs. We had a standard routine: the person who had the most recent birthday celebration was in charge of the next sign-on-the-lawn activity.

Thus, at 7 a.m. or so on a member's birthday, she could look out and see a gigantic, two-piece 5-0 sign, with balloons attached, on her lawn. A group of six or seven Club '43 members would serenade the celebrant in an inept version of "Happy Birthday" before the gang took off for work or breakfast at the nearest diner. The sign would remain on the lawn all day. Passing drivers would honk their horns and yell such things as "You are old." Westfielders became quite familiar with the big 5-0 as it made its appearance a lot that year on town lawns.

For our 50th birthday year, we shunned our 40th-birthday spa shirts and donned new tee-shirts---green ones featuring the chemical formula for estrogen. After all, we had moved into a chronological period that deemed us interested parties in the estrogen arena. (We argued about the message that would go on the shirts; one person suggested we put the list of all of the colleges our children were attending at the time, to show how tuition-poor we were).

On the back of the shirts, we had our individual numbers— actually, every one of us got number 43 to dovetail with our team's name and birth year!

We scheduled a number of activities, starting with a lecture on women's health courtesy of Dr. Herald. Member Diana McGonigle, a nurse, hosted the event attended by many of our friends who shared an interest in such topics as estrogen replacement medicine. (The message: take it).

And we had another softball game, with younger Westfield female friends as opponents. The game garnered a bit of publicity- --several days before the event, The Westfield Leader featured a front-page picture of a group of Club '43 members dressed in our matching hats and shirts, all with number 43.

Even the talent of opposition pitcher Eva Wiley could not shut us down completely; we were still pretty athletic for half-centenarians. But the celebratory antics of some Club '43 members determined our fate.

At one point, with the score tied, a batter for the opponents' team hit a ball into the infield. Our pitcher, Linnea Rhodes, bobbled the ball a bit as she grabbed for it; the throw to our first baseman (or is it first basewoman?) Patty Noerr was not on time and the batter smiled as she stood on first.

The next opposition batter also lopped a ball toward the mound; this time, Linnea fielded it with professional-like ease and tossed the ball on target to Patty at first. With that, Linnea and Patty started to celebrate their deft handling of the ball and the resulting out. They high-fived each other and engaged in a bit of a celebration-like dance.

What they forgot was that the woman who had been on first now was circling the other bases. From my shortstop post, I was screaming at my pair of teammates, as were fellow Club '43 players on and off the field.

It was too late---the runner touched home plate.

We lost by a run.

To this day, every time I see Linnea Rhodes, I remind her of that game.

Individually, we Club '43 stalwarts each celebrated our 50th natal days; my husband and three children entertained for me at a "half-a-hundred" celebration with about 75 guests.

Our 50th birthdays also were marked as a group late in 1993 at a dinner where we exchanged gifts.

Overall, we had a most enjoyable---and fun---year.

Then we took a break---until the next milestone festivities.

The 60th Birthday

In early 2003, I contacted some Club '43 members and invited them to my home to plan for our 60th birthdays that year. Six of us sat around my dining room table, sipped good wine furnished by my spouse, John, and mulled our celebration options. We christened ourselves the Club '43 officers for the year, with yours truly assuming the presidency (because I called the meeting!) and the others taking on varied offices.

Today, when I think about the conversation that evening, I still remain shocked.

I recall suggesting to the others that we might scrap the baseball game that had been part of our 40th and 50th birthday festivities and do something "philanthropic," such as sponsoring a simple fundraiser of some sort.

"Raise money for what?" asked Linnea Rhodes.

So I turned to Judi Thompson, who was sitting on my left.

"I thought maybe we could raise some money for beast cancer research because, as I recall, you had breast cancer, right?"

Judi said: "Yes---twice."

The others looked at me but said nothing at first.

Then Loretta Wilson, seated to Judi's left, said: "I've had breast cancer, too."

Before I could respond, Lesley Robins, sitting next to Loretta, blurted out:" So have I."

I was about to express my shock that all three were cancer survivors, when Diana McGonigle, seated next to Lesley, remarked: "I've never said much about it, but I had breast cancer, too."

As I recall, I headed straight for the kitchen and another glass of Pinot Noir. Linnea Rhodes was right on my heels. Our faces expressed our bewilderment: Four of our six officers have had breast cancer? Linnea and I decided we better commit ourselves to doing something for the cause. After all, we were seeing the statistics right before our eyes.

A few weeks later, we gathered together Club '43 members; our numbers had dwindled to 12 because some had moved out of town in the preceding decade or others chose not to be active for the 60th birthday observances. Thus, we proceeded without some of our charter members, including Patty Noerr, who was planning to retire from her teaching post and move out of town.

The 12 of us decided that, if we each could somehow raise $500, we would have $6,000 to donate to a breast cancer cause and we would not be taxing ourselves in the effort.

Thus began our plans for "60 for 60," a unique walk to raise monies for the local Susan Komen Foundation organization. The "60 for 60" name refers to our objective of walking 60 times around the bandstand at Mindowaskin Park in downtown Westfield in honor of our 60th birthdays. Now the distance, even at 60 times, would not tax any exercise-prone individual. In our case, we decided to add up the walks of each one, so that really five times around would be enough per person! Color us inventive but lazy!

The planning was fun---we met periodically at my home and, over some food and wine, divided the tasks and made our plans. Susan Carovillano arrived one night with shirts and hats, a donation from her firm, British Petroleum. Judi Thompson, our club treasurer, handled any checks we received for deposit in a special account for our walk. Realtor Mary McEnerney had a large sign made for the day---it looked perfect at Mindowaskin Park. Linnea Rhodes helped to keep the e-mails up to date. Others handled publicity, or negotiations with the town for the use of the park, or whatever. We each got a job of some sort.

The last meeting at my home came just a week before the event. Linnea, who thrives on organization, convinced me to set a "rule" that we would not drink wine until we settled some important final plans for the walk, including insurance issues. I announced my "rule" at the outset of the meeting. With that, I heard a unison response of "Baloney." My guests were opening the wine bottles as we moved right ahead and settled the plans.

We had sent out letters to friends and asked them to sponsor us on our short walk. We met our original goal within days, and by the time the walk came on Sept. 23, 2003, we had raised more than $15,000. The Komen staff was thrilled and honored us a month or so later.

Upon hearing about our group, News 12 New Jersey's Della Crews devoted one of her half-hour "Defying Age" shows to Club '43. Six of us appeared on the show that even featured a clip from a movie, made in the 60s, featuring member Cathy Rock---then a Dominican nun in Chicago.

Member Charlotte Clevenger hosted a spring brunch for Club '43 to celebrate her 60th birthday. Most of us marked our individual birthdays in other ways. In my case, some friends surprised me (two months before my birthday) at Monmouth Racetrack and even had a race named after me there! I relish the photos of yours truly and the others in the winners' circle. (I bought a ticket for every horse in the race so I would have a winning ticket to keep!).

Throughout the year, as each Club '43 member celebrated her 60th birthday, all of the others sent cards and e-mails. We kept in touch through e-mails, phone calls, and our planning meetings for "60 for 60." By the end of 2003, we were talking about our next big year---2013---when we will celebrate our 70th birthdays!

Club '43 Baseball Teams

40th year (1983)

50th year (1993)

Club '43   50th Year

Birthday celebration on Diana McGonigle's front lawn

Outing to Monmouth Park Race Track

Club '43 60th Year

Back row from left: Tina Lesher, Penny Dinger, Loretta Wilson, Madeleine Sullivan

Middle row: Susan Carovillano, Mary McEnerney, Linnea Rhodes, Judi Thompson

Front row: Charlotte Clevenger, Lesley Robins, Cathy Rock, Diana McGonigle

Susan Bakum Carovillano

It was 1980 and the younger of Susan Carovillano's two sons was in second grade. Susan decided it was time to return to teaching physical education and applied to a high school which she had left a number of years before to raise her children. At that time, the school and most others in America lacked girls' varsity teams, so Susan had never had an opportunity to coach outside of intramurals.

Now, with Title XI having opened up the sports ranks to young women, Susan was eager to return to work and to coach. She was cognizant that the market for teaching jobs had tightened because female teachers---once forced or expected to leave permanently when they had children---now were keeping their positions.

When Susan was informed that her former district had an opening, though, she figured she was a shoo-in to return to the high school there.

After all, "they knew me," she says. "I thought they liked me."

But she was not hired.

"They gave the job to some kid right out of college---I think it was a board member's friend or relative," she states.

To Susan, the message was "loud and clear."

She moved into the corporate sector.

***

When Club '43 held its "60 for 60 Walk" fundraiser for breast cancer research at Mindowaskin Park in September 2003, among the participants was Susan Carovillano's mother, Josephine Bakum.

At 88, she walked briskly, exhibiting her emphasis on keeping active; to this day she works out daily at a local gym. She also walked with pride; after all, Josephine twice had survived breast cancer---the first time at age 85.

Josephine is the second oldest of six children born to Italian immigrants. After finishing Rahway High School, she entered Beth Israel Hospital's nursing program in Newark.

"My mother was unique," contends Susan. "To be a child of immigrants and have a profession as a registered nurse---that was something."

Through a physician-friend, Josephine was introduced to Walter Bakum, a Newark native who taught history and coached basketball at the city's Westside High. Walter had been a basketball star at Southside, another of Newark's high schools, and had been offered full scholarships to Georgetown and George Washington University. He chose Georgetown; while a freshman there, he suffered pneumonia and was admitted to George Washington University Hospital.

"The story is that GWU then recruited him away," laughs his daughter, Susan.

Walter played on the GWU basketball squad whose team manager was Red Auerbach, later to become the heralded general manager of the Boston Celtics. Calvin Griffiths, who would become owner of the Washington Senators, a major league baseball team, also was a friend of Walter Bakum during their undergraduate days.

After briefly playing professional basketball, Walter began a successful career as teacher/coach at Westside; his players included Richie Regan, who starred at Seton Hall, where he eventually became athletic director.

When Walter passed away from cancer at age 70, he had what Susan terms "an amazing funeral." Many of his ex-students/players described how Walter Bakum had made a difference in their lives. Residents of Clark, N. J., where Walter had served as a Board of Education member for more than a quarter-century, also lavished praise; the town even named a gymnasium after him.

"His legacy is not money, "says Susan Carovillano, citing the scores of newspaper articles that focus on her father. "My father felt he had a contribution to make and he helped so many students and others along the way. He helped me become what I am today."

***

Susan grew up in Clark, a town adjacent to Westfield. The Bakum home, a 1950s ranch-style house, was typical of those constructed in developments in what once was farmland. For many settlers who came from Newark, about 10 miles away, Clark represented a new world---suburbia.

The typical Clark mother was home with her children, and Josephine was no exception.

"My mother did not go to work until my youngest brother was in sixth grade," says Susan, the oldest of three children. "Then she worked part-time at Beth Israel Hospital. Later she worked as a school nurse until her retirement."

Susan was not yet 3 years old when her mother put her in ballet class two days a week. The instructor, Elsa Heilich, taught classical ballet and toe at the Elks Club in Rahway, just across the border from Clark. Susan took classes for more than a decade, even commuting by bus to the city of Elizabeth, the county seat, after the classes were switched there.

"Dancing was the thing for girls then," recalls Susan. "We had no soccer like they have today. It was all about dancing."

Susan spent her grade school days at St. John's in Clark, but when it came time for high school, she opted for Arthur Johnson Regional.

"The nuns were upset that I did not want to go to a Catholic school," says Susan.

High school, she admitted, interfered with her dancing pursuits. She participated in the lone high school-level athletic pursuits open to young women in the early 60s---intramurals and cheerleading. For the latter, she won her varsity letter. Cheerleading, she emphasized, was the only way a female student could pursue that coveted varsity letter that would adorn her school sweater.

***

When it came time for college studies, Susan interviewed at Montclair State, about 20 miles north of Clark. She intended to study history as an entrée to teaching.

"Let's face it," says Susan, echoing the sentiment of many her age. "Women did not have a lot of choices. Be a nurse, a teacher, or go to Katharine Gibbs (Secretarial School)."

While at her Montclair interview, though, Susan met some physical education teachers---and changed her mind about a major.

Montclair State's Panzer School of Physical Education was a premier institution of its kind and offered a lot of leadership-type studies; it also prepared enrollees for education careers, if they so desired.

To this day, Susan will argue--- to those who ask her why she took phys ed---that her studies were more like pre-med.

"We had a very heavy emphasis on science plus liberal arts," she says. "Most of the students had been really good high school students. The department was selective."

College in the 60s translated to some never-forgotten moments in history.

"I was riveted during the Cuban missile crisis," Susan states about the October 1962 period when President John F. Kennedy dealt with halting the Soviet Union's construction of missile bases in Cuba.

Montclair State was home to many young veterans studying on the GI Bill

"They were getting called up," she says. "It was scary because they were students at our college."

And, like others in Club '43, she remembers when President Kennedy was assassinated in 1963 in Dallas. A professor came into Susan's class and delivered the sad news. The university shut down immediately to join a period of mourning in the country.

It was at a Montclair State sorority-fraternity mixer that Susan met Jim Carovillano. By any stretch of the imagination, the Air Force veteran was a BMOC---Big Man on Campus. The Rutherford, N.J. native was captain of the undefeated Montclair State football team and of the baseball team.

"I was pinned in college," says Susan, alluding to the historical tradition of a young man giving his fraternity pin for his girlfriend to wear. "At that time, unlike today, if you were not hooked up with someone, you were dead meat."

***

Susan set out on a career path to teach physical education and health. She had completed her student teaching at Governor Livingston High School, Berkeley Heights, N. J., and took a fulltime post there after receiving her college degree. Her sports coaching was limited to intramurals because the school had no girls' varsity teams.

A year later, after she and Jim exchanged wedding vows, Susan followed her spouse to Cortland, N.Y., where he pursued his master's degree and also coached. Susan taught at a nearby elementary school. Teaching in a university town proved interesting to Susan after her New Jersey experience.

"Gov. (Nelson) Rockefeller gave a ton of money...public schools were miles ahead in resources," she says.

The Carovillanos returned to the Garden State after Jim completed graduate studies and began his teaching/coaching career; today he is a school principal in Clark, Susan's hometown. Susan also had a number of teaching opportunities and accepted a job as a physical education teacher at a local high school.

***

For Club '43 members, the memories of the so-called Vietnam conflict are etched in their minds. America, with its long-recognized position of being available to help out against the plight of those faced with Communism, engaged in a years-long battle to stop the North Vietnamese attack on South Vietnam. Many friends and relatives of Club '43 members served in Vietnam or in service during that period. Close to 60,000 Americans, mostly young men, lost their lives in that land a half-world away.

"It seemed every day in the papers I would read about someone I went to high school with or I dated or Jim knew---they were dying in Vietnam," says Susan. "Then his brother..."

Bob Carovillano had left college and headed to Officer Candidate School. His life ended when he was only 20 in a helicopter accident in Vietnam.

"I cannot describe to you what it was like the day Jim's uncle came to our home to break the news," says Susan. "Oh, my God..."

Susan believes that the Vietnam War impacted the political feelings of those her age. It certainly colored her perspective.

"When I tell people why I am opposed to Iraq, I tell them my brother-in-law was killed in Vietnam."

***

When her return to teaching did not materialize, Susan decided to venture into new working territory. A friend, Nancy Brandt, told Susan about a program, at nearby Kean College, for women returning to the workforce.

"Nancy talked me into going there," says Susan, who ended up taking a job at Lincoln Federal Savings in downtown Westfield, close to the schools where her sons, Jeffrey and Brian, were enrolled.

"I was hired to start a training department," she explains," so I moved from school teaching to the business world."

In building the corporate education department at the bank, Susan established and taught courses for tellers, supervisors, managers, etc.

By becoming involved in the corporate education community, Susan was able to gain a reputation in her specialty. She moved on to the large insurance company, Chubb, where she again used her teaching background to oversee professional development courses.

Today, Susan is an integral part of the organizational and learning professional team at BP, the world's third largest oil company. She works out of Wayne, N.J. as part of an international team that assesses the organizational needs of the employees in the company's Western Hemisphere division and designs appropriate training/development curriculum.

"It's the best job I've had and for the best company," says Susan. "I feel valued and appreciated. I work with a good group of professionals who constantly share ideas."

Her company offices are located next to a building that is part of the campus of William Paterson University, where fellow Club '43 member Tina Lesher is employed.

Through an introduction by Tina, Susan met university development representatives and has been instrumental over the years in securing large donations to WPU from BP. As Tina has said repeatedly, "it's all because of Club '43."

***

Susan maintains that corporate life has changed over the years for those who ascend its ranks.

"People are working harder than ever. In the old days, you had secretaries. No more. You get e-mails, conference calls—it is so different."

Unlike in decades before, though, companies are not pushing married women with children out the door.

"When we get a talented woman, we accommodate her," says Susan, referring to the 21st century practices of telecommuting and shared jobs.

And how would Susan describe her own career path?

"I was never scared to move on!"

Susan plans to do that, as she mulls a professional move into the consulting ranks in the near future. This should provide her more time to enjoy her role as a grandmother and as a concerned daughter whose mother, Josephine, again has battled breast cancer.

In addition to spending weekends at a shore home, Susan has taken her athletic skills to the golf course.

"Maybe," she says, "I finally will have enough time to get serious about that game."

Susan Carovillano

Baby with parents (1943)
Sorority Cotillion (1963)
Cheerleader with father (1960)
With family and mother (2005)

Charlotte Skoda Clevenger

Charlotte Skoda Clevenger laughs---and she has an infectious laugh---when her thoughts return to 1962 and her job at Western Reserve Medical School in her native Cleveland.

"They act today like it's revolutionary," she says about embryo stem cell research. "But it's been going on for years."

Charlotte left Kent State University after a year of study ("my father said if you are not going to be a nurse or teacher, don't go to college") and landed "a secretarial lab job" at the medical school.

"I became a lab assistant, really," she says. "It was definitely on-the-job training. And I didn't make any money!"

In addition to "putting things in petri dishes," Charlotte says the doctors would send her from the lab to the nearby hospital's delivery rooms to get blood from placentas.

"We'd study it," she says, adding that the physicians at the lab also would freeze embryos for research, test chromosomes for sexual dysfunction tests, and do amniocentesis on pregnant women.

Thus, the debate on stem cell research, so prevalent in the 21 century, is old news to Charlotte.

"We were doing a lot of it in the early 60s," she smiles. "I just never really thought about it."

***

Charlotte's parents, Gabriella and Frank Skoda, were first-generation Americans of German and Slovenian descent. They both grew up in the "old neighborhood" around St. Clair and Euclid Avenues in Cleveland.

"I just found out a year ago," says Charlotte, "that my paternal grandmother died during childbirth---actually, during an abortion."

Charlotte claims her father and his sister were treated shabbily by her grandfather and his second wife.

"So my father made his own way---delivering papers and living with his other grandmother at a boarding house."

Charlotte's maternal grandparents had a big difference in their ages---she was 15 and he 40 when they wed.

"My maternal grandmother never spoke English," says Charlotte, "only Slovenian."

Charlotte wanted to learn that language and asked her mother, who had learned Slovenian at home, to teach her.

"'You don't need that,' my mother said. So I never learned."

The family---Charlotte, her older brother, Frank Joseph, and their parents---lived downstairs in a two-family house they owned in the old neighborhood; they rented the upstairs unit.

Charlotte's parents only made it to the eighth grade. Frank Skoda worked all his life in blue-collar jobs, though he did eventually take courses that enabled him to work in the air conditioning and heating business. Her mother never worked, but, Charlotte says, "always did stuff for the Catholic church. And my parents had lots of friends."

At Collinwood High School in northeast Cleveland, Charlotte was a member of the school's first group of high steppers, young women who donned majorette hats and outfits and entertained with varied routines at football halftime shows.

Cleveland in the 1950s and 1960s was far different from it current status.

"It was fascinating downtown with lots of shops and streetcars. My mother did not drive but we could walk to town and shop. I thought it was fascinating."

***

Wayne Clevenger was a Western Reserve University undergraduate when he was introduced to Charlotte Skoda by a friend who also attended the school. Through Charlotte, Wayne secured a job at the lab where she worked.

His task?

"He counted chromosomes," laughs Charlotte.

The pair married in September 1965. A month later, Charlotte was driving their 1960 Buick on a "rainy, cold night" and a drunken driver plowed into her car. With the insurance money, she purchased a new 1966 Mustang.

Wayne began working the second shift---3 p.m. to 3 a.m.---as a foreman at Ford Motor Co.

"I would give him dinner at 3 a.m.," recalls Charlotte, "and then go back to bed and get up and go to work."

One night, in December 1965, Charlotte was home alone when she heard a knock on the door. She opened it to find a person bearing a special delivery letter.

"Oh my God," she remembers saying.

The letter was a draft notice, telling Wayne to report for duty the first week of January.

"I called my mother and his mother; we were all crying," says Charlotte.

She figured Wayne would be going to Vietnam, where the conflict was heating up. Wayne, too, was shocked by his call-up notice, and though he was eligible to pursue officers' training, he opted for the enlisted ranks. When her spouse departed for basic training in Georgia, Charlotte remained behind in Ohio.

In August 1966, she joined him at Fort Gordon.

"Wayne had called and said he was coming home that weekend and we'd drive back together."

That is how they moved to Augusta, Ga.---with their Mustang filled up with needed belongings.

"Just enough to get by," says Charlotte. "Four knives, four forks..."

Wayne had told his bride that they would be moving into an apartment being vacated by a soldier about to be shipped out. But it turned out that the GI did not leave his assignment, and the Clevengers arrived with no place to live.

They perused newspaper ads for a few hours and went to see a trailer that was available. Charlotte described it as "a filthy, dirty, pig sty---awful."

They moved in.

"My husband loved it," says Charlotte, about their new home in Crystal Springs Trailer Park on the famous US 1 that runs through the South. "He said 'these will be the best years of our life.'"

"Best years? I will never forget the one-and-a half years we lived there," says Charlotte, as she describes her life at the trailer park:

"We had a car so we took people to the store...people asked for money; we were like the bank...the neighbors had 20 cats preying all over the place...it was like a tin can in the summer. We got the manager to give us an air conditioner---for a price...in the winter it was freezing cold. We were always running out of fuel...there was no grass. All clay. So we had to swab it on weekends..."

Charlotte took the Civil Service test and got a job in the supply room of the base's closed-circuit TV department. Wayne and his fellow soldiers had formation every day where, Charlotte reports, "they picked out guys" to head to Vietnam.

Wayne escaped that fate and the couple returned to Cleveland after his Army stint ended in 1968.

***

It was back south for Charlotte and Wayne two years later, when he was transferred to Sumter, S.C., where he worked initially as personnel manager for a battery company, and then for five years as its plant manager. Their son, Patrick, was a year old when they made the move; their daughter, Lisa, was born while they resided in Sumter.

The civil rights movement was active at the time, and Charlotte clearly remembers the mantra of Southerners about how blacks were treated there as opposed to the north: "We keep 'em quiet down here; you rile 'em up up there."

"I could never understand those Southern people," says Charlotte.

Sumter, in Charlotte's mind, was a tiny 60s country town replete with one theatre and two department stories. She and her family lived in a development, the new trend in American living.

"It was a few houses in an open field."

Like the average family at that time, the Clevengers had one car, so Charlotte would drive Wayne to work and even drove him home for lunch. They remained in South Carolina for eight years and, Charlotte says, had she not met women friends through the Newcomers Club, she would have been plain "bored" for that period of time.

The Clevengers' next stop was Yardley, Pa. The move came in January 1978 and the "kids had no winter clothes." Wayne commuted to Philadelphia, so there was "no more coming home for lunch," says Charlotte. Two years later, they moved to Westfield, where they have resided ever since.

***

Unlike her colleagues in Club '43, Charlotte did not focus on a career. She did work six months at Sealfons, a popular children's clothing store in Westfield, and six months part-time at an eye doctor's office.

But Wayne "thought it was stupid---he gave me no real support about working," says Charlotte in an amusing way.

So she assumed the role she still has---that of homemaker.

Within that role, though, Charlotte had made her mark in volunteer service, from teaching religious education to working with the Girl Scouts, etc. For years she has been a stalwart volunteer in the linen room at the Children Specialized Hospital in Mountainside, a town that adjoins Westfield. She plays in bridge groups and is an active tennis player. She and Wayne, who received his MBA from Columbia and now works in the venture capital field, also have four grandchildren. They have enjoyed traveling to Europe and other interesting destinations over the years. The Clevengers enjoy good wines---"it's a long way from that Thunderbird stuff," says Charlotte.

She refers to Club '43 as a "fun" group, and gets a kick out of telling others about the organization.

"People cannot believe that I am in a club that really does not do anything else for 10 years in between our big birthdays!

***

Today, according to Charlotte, her beloved downtown Cleveland is "dead," mirroring many American cities now consumed with "malls and everything." Charlotte makes that observation with credibility. She keeps in touch with her high school friends. And, though they reside hundreds of miles away in New Jersey, Charlotte and Wayne have season tickets to the Cleveland Browns and attend all of the team's home games. Charlotte fondly concedes that, despite enjoying life in colonial Westfield, she still has a bit of "that old neighborhood" in her.

Charlotte Clevenger

At 13 months (1944)
Bride (1965)
Dressed for church (1950)
At a Paris café (2004)

Penny
Vanderbilt Dinger

Elevating her conversation almost to a philosophical level, Penny Vanderbilt Dinger can clearly elucidate how life is tied so closely to the time period of one's birth.

"The things that shaped my personality," she argues, "would not have impacted me if I were born today."

Penny cites a number of examples to prove her point.

As a young child, she had what is known as a "lazy eye" and thus wore glasses as well as a patch over one eye. (Penny would lie to her aunt when the latter asked if her niece was wearing her glasses all of the time. To this day, Penny is a bit guilty about not telling the truth.) At age 6, Penny was sent to Columbia Presbyterian Hospital in Manhattan for eye surgery to correct the problem. In those days, as she points out to make her case, parents were not allowed to stay with a child as is the case in many hospitals today.

She still shakes her head as she recounts the hospital experience.

"I was put in a crib---can you believe that? And I felt I was just left there by my family."

Had it been her children or grandchildren in the hospital today, the situation would be totally different.

Fast forward to the days when, as a 19-year-old bride, Penny took birth-control pills when they were fairly new to the market.

"They were 10 times worse than now. Not like what they give you today."

And when she talks about her first divorce, the twice-married Penny also reflects on the differences in the generations.

"Today, I wouldn't do it. We would have had counseling. "

Penny claims her whole life has been characterized by examples such as the aforementioned.

"If I were born today, these would be non-issues. I look back at the things that affected me and know that it would be different had they happened today."

***

When your father's name is Cornelius Vanderbilt, you expect people to assume you are wealthy.

"I guess we must be related in some way," says Penny about the famed industrial baron of the early 20th century. My father---also Cornelius Vanderbilt---kidded that we were the bastard side of the family."

Her father owned a construction firm, and Penny was raised in an "upper-middle class" family, with a nice Staten Island home and country club membership.

Though they were Episcopalian, the Vanderbilts sent Penny, the second of four children, to a Catholic kindergarten.

"I was a non-Catholic. I felt like an outsider, even though I was only 5. Nobody liked me. I think it was discrimination."

For grade school, she moved to Staten Island's PS 42, part of the New York City public school system. Each class had more than 40 students. Penny recalls the taunting lyrics of a ditty sung by rivals at PS8: "All the monkeys in the zoo go to PS 42."

Having buck teeth didn't add to Penny's self-esteem.

"I was 11 or 12 before I got braces. I wouldn't have waited that long if my own kids needed to correct something like that."

She skipped seventh grade---not because she was a budding academic star.

"The class was overcrowded so three of us were just skipped into eighth grade."

For Penny, missing seventh grade has had an effect on her to this day.

"That's when you learn all about grammar. I still don't know good grammar. I have trouble with things like apostrophes."

As a result of her abbreviated grade school education, Penny entered high school at Staten Island Academy when she was 12. She is candid in describing being a high school freshman at that age: "I was physically and emotionally too young. I had no social skills. I still had braces."

Girls had to wear skirts at Staten Island Academy, a coed school.

"If you wore sneakers, you had to stay after school," Penny remembers.

At the outset, she was shy in her class of 34 students. Sports assumed an important part of her academy life, as she became active in varsity field hockey and tennis. She also played forward on the school basketball team in an era when there were six on a team: three forwards on one side of the court and the three defensive guards on the other. (Players could not cross the line, and could only dribble twice before stopping or passing the ball).

Like many of her friends, she took up smoking.

"I don't know if I would do that today," says Penny, now a non-smoker.

Penny never learned how to study, because she really never had to do much of it in grade school. So she got by at Staten Island Academy by reading on the bus on the way to school and wound up mostly with Cs on her report card.

Still, her parents thought she would have no problem getting into their alma mater---Cornell, an Ivy League institution. So when Penny was not accepted at Cornell, she stayed home and entered Wagner College on Staten Island.

***

The driving age in New York in 1960 was 18, so 16-year-old college freshman Penny Vanderbilt took three buses and then walked up a hill to the Wagner campus. She majored in math ("I didn't know grammar so math was a good major") and "did OK" in school. Other than playing tennis, she participated little in the way of college activities at Wagner.

She was headed back to Wagner for her sophomore year when, in August 1961, she was introduced to a Maine college by a placement staffer who was a friend of Penny's mother, Lillian.

Nasson College, a liberal arts institution with 500 students, had just been accredited. Penny visited the campus---and decided to transfer there.

"I was so homesick at first," she recalls. "I had teeth marks on my lip so I would not cry. But I got over that."

Academically, she did well as a transfer math major and even made the Dean's List.

"In chemistry class, I once let two guys copy my work. They got Bs and I got a C. The professor was wise to us."

***

Nasson College was located in Springvale, Me., about 40 miles south of Portland.

'The winters were long and cold. There was a lot of poverty there," Penny says. "People went hunting---not for the sport."

She applied and was accepted for her junior year at "bigger schools," including Penn State and Michigan State. Nevertheless, she decided to return to Nasson. Unlike sophomore year, when she resided in a dormitory, Penny moved into a college-owned house with more than 20 other students. She also had her own car---a gift from her aunt.

That Fall, she began dating fellow student Bill Crandall, a Rhode Island native. The whirlwind romance culminated with the pair's decision to get a marriage license over Thanksgiving break.

She and Bill drove to Elkton, Md., the East Coast town of choice for getting quick marriage licenses in those days; they obtained the license but did not tie the knot. The next day---the Wednesday before Thanksgiving---they drove to Staten Island to join the Vanderbilt family for the holiday. Penny had no intention of mentioning the license to her parents. That evening, Bill joined the family at dinner at the club to which the Vanderbilts belonged.

"My parents gave him the third degree about his family, etc." says Penny. "He did well."

When they returned later that evening to the Vanderbilt home, Penny's parents confronted them about the marriage license. It turned out that Penny's college roommate had called Lillian to alert her that her daughter had headed to Maryland for the license.

The Vanderbilts wanted Penny to wait before taking the marital plunge. In the end, they agreed to the marriage---if Penny and Bill had an appropriate wedding. When Bill's mother was informed about the impending nuptials, she asked: "Is she pregnant?"

"Now I think I probably would ask the same thing if it were one of my children," says Penny.

Six weeks later, Penny, age 19, and Bill were married in Staten Island. The reception was held at the well-appointed Vanderbilt home.

"My mother redecorated in six weeks," smiles Penny.

***

Back at school in Springvale, the couple moved into a small apartment; Bill took a job loading trucks to help pay the bills. Penny claims she was depressed, attributing her state of mind to the "strong" birth control pills she was prescribed. That summer---before senior year---the Crandalls lived in Staten Island, in an apartment vacated for the summer by a relative. While Bill toiled as a laborer at his father-in-law's company, Penny sold Avon products.

"I hated it," she states about selling door-to-door. "I would ring and run. Bill would deliver the stuff for me. I did hit up a lot of relatives to buy Avon."

The couple returned to Nasson for their final year. By the start of spring semester, when she was 13 ½ credits shy of her bachelor's degree, Penny left school.

"I just quit. I couldn't sit in class. I was nervous."

While Bill was awarded his bachelor's degree, Penny settled for an associates degree. Bill began interviewing with Mass Mutual; for the final interview, Penny was asked to accompany him.

"Here I was with the heebie-jeebies and his job was on the line," says Penny.

Bill was hired--- as a group sales representative---and the Crandalls moved to an apartment in Staten Island. They became parents for the first time on Dec. 31, 1964, with the birth of son Roger.

"I was petrified of having the baby," says Penny. "Fathers were not allowed in the delivery room then."

As Bill's career escalated, Penny remained a homemaker. They bought a home in Staten Island, and had two more children, daughters Ginger and Merry. Then the Crandalls moved to a large home in Maplewood, N.J.

Penny tried to emulate the life of a woman who did not need to work. She joined a tennis club; that provided a slice of social life for her. But when the children were in school, she found herself bored.

"I didn't know what to do with myself."

If it were today, she sighs, "I would have gotten a job, but back then I assumed the man supports the family and I didn't really have to work."

Her solution?

"I got a divorce."

***

Her three children ranged in age from 6 to 13 when Penny Vanderbilt Crandall took the divorce route. Without counseling or an attempt to save the union, she made up her mind to leave the marriage.

She says today that she thought Bill was not happy in the marriage and that "we had our problems. I thought I was doing the right thing."

Her family questioned her decision. And shortly thereafter, her mother died of a brain tumor.

"You know, she worked hard," says Penny about Lillian Vanderbilt, "although she was a homemaker. Physically, women had more to do at home---preparing big meals for families, putting the wash on clothes lines, things like that. My mother also did volunteer work and late in life got her master's at NYU."

Penny went through with the divorce; today, almost 30 years later, she reiterates that she probably would not have done so had counseling been prevalent at the time.

She was 34 and on her own. She remained with the children in the Maplewood home and Bill took a small apartment. On weekends, he would move into the house to be with the children and she would go stay in his apartment.

"It got weird," she says, "especially when his girlfriend would come along with him."

Penny still did not move into the job market because she preferred to be with the children. Then she became involved with an older man whom she helped care for as he fought what turned out to be a fatal bout with cancer.

"My kids hated him---and they probably hated me at that point," says Penny.

When she was about 37, she ventured into the working world at her family's Staten Island business. Though she "had no confidence" in herself, she assumed a number of bookkeeping-related duties and began to realize that she could handle the work.

She met a fellow employee---a sales rep named August (Gus) Dinger, whom she wed after he had left the company for another job. At age 39, she gave birth to their son, August Jr.

"So in terms of Club '43 members, I have the oldest and the youngest of all our children," Penny notes.

Gus Dinger joined with Penny's younger brother, Michael Vanderbilt, in owning and operating Jiffy Lube franchises. He and Penny bought the Maplewood home after Bill Crandall gave them a good price for his share of it.

Then, in 1988, tragedy hit the Vanderbilt family when Penny's father, Cornelius, was stabbed to death while he was at home.

The case still has not been solved, and Penny surmises that the attacker may have been someone her father knew.

The marriage to Gus Dinger has been characterized by Penny as one in which she and her spouse were "in different worlds." After eight years, they divorced. Penny took some money she had inherited and bought out Gus from the Jiffy Lube partnership.

"I had to take a 10-year buyout," she explains, adding that she also became sole owner of her Maplewood house after paying Gus for his half.

***

Now, as a partner in the Jiffy Lube business---she and Michael own three locations in Central New Jersey---Penny works primarily with payroll, insurance and other bookkeeping duties.

"I can support myself," she states.

She harbors no thoughts of retiring: "I cannot do that unless I sell the business."

Her "sanity," she claims, comes from two of her athletic passions---paddle tennis and golf. She moved several years ago to a home close to Echo Lake Country Club, where Penny became one of the first women to secure full membership in the club. She is one of the top players on Echo Lake's paddle tennis teams, and regularly scores in the 90s in golf. She even recorded a hole-in-one while playing in a Jiffy Lube golf tournament in California.

With her other siblings (brother Neil and sister Sue Moran) and some of her grandchildren in the area, Penny gets to spend a lot of time with family members. To those who have watched her organize a creative social event, or outplay others on the paddle court or golf course, she appears to be the model of confidence.

She disagrees: "I am still not a confident person."

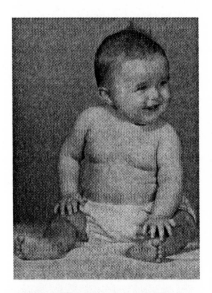

Penny Dinger

Baby (1944)
High school grad (1960)
Bathing beauty (1950)
Business woman (1999)

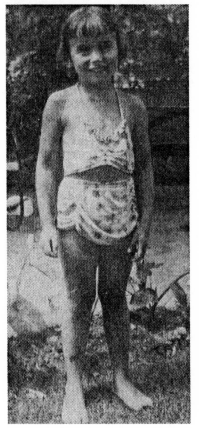

Tina Rodgers Lesher

For more than a year, members of the American Newspaper Guild at The Scrantonian-Scranton Tribune had worked without a contract. Negotiations were ongoing between the publishers and the union's all-male team. Finally, in 1968, a salary deal was struck.

Tina Rodgers had joined the 27-member newsroom staff two years before, right out of the master's program at the University of Missouri School of Journalism. She served as assistant women's editor; her superior, veteran society editor Gene Brislin, was the only other woman on staff. By virtue of their posts, both had journeyman status in the Guild.

When the contract deal was finalized, those who handled editing got $5-a-week increments in addition to the regular raises. That is, all the male editors were given the additional few dollars---but not the two women.

"Gene was angry," says Tina. "So we marched into the office of the managing editor and quit. Gene knew they would never let her go because not only was she good but she was married to the paper's Pulitzer Prize-winning reporter."

The managing editor, an ex-Guild member himself, said he could not believe "the men did that to you two." So he phoned the publisher and got permission to boost the two women's salaries by $10-a-week for editing, twice what the men would get.

More than 35 years later, Dr. Tina Rodgers Lesher, now a journalism professor, will argue that the salary discrimination continues, even in an era of equality.

"It was rampant in my own department at a public university at the time I was hired in 1989," she says. "Men were given higher salaries by men for no solid reason. Admittedly, the situation has improved in some sectors. But, in many cases, as the women in our department have argued formally even of late, it has not changed. I will never understand why."

***

Tina Rodgers was raised in Dunmore, Pa., a borough adjacent to the city of Scranton.

At her christening, her godparents gave her the name Alice after her mother, the former Alice Bridget Fitzsimmons. To avoid the confusion of two in the family with the same first name, the baby Alice was given the nickname "Tina." The name Alice remains on all legal documents, however, from her license to her passport.

"If someone calls me Alice today, I figure it must be a bill collector," says Tina, the third of four children born to Alice and her husband, Hugh J. Rodgers, who headed a trucking company and a tire business.

Tina was the first in her family to attend kindergarten.

"One of the neighbors was in my class and his family's chauffeur drove us to school every day ---in a limousine. I tell my friends that and they say---come on, in Dunmore? You went to school in a limousine?"

Tina spent her grade school years at St. Paul's School in Scranton, where the average class size was about 70.

"I used to chuckle at PTA meetings in Westfield when parents would complain that their kids' classes had more than 25 students."

Tina recalls the interest at St. Paul's in raising money for "pagan babies."

"We'd save pennies and when we got to $5, we could name a pagan baby who was going to be converted to Catholicism, I guess. Years later, during the Vietnam War, we often wonder if those babies were shooting our friends."

To this day, Tina claims that the best education she ever received was in grade school at St. Paul's, despite the large class sizes.

"I forever am grateful to the nuns for teaching me the basics of grammar and how to write and think," says Tina. "I realize they also taught me a lot about the ways to approach teaching---be fair but demanding, and know what you are talking about. I believe I have adapted that approach in my role as a professor."

***

The Scranton area was "a great place to grow up," according to Tina, who had many relatives there. Tina's father and his friends had a hunting lodge in the Poconos ("I do not think they hunted a lot") and she harbors memories of spending Sundays with other families there and engaging in clay pigeon shooting and horseback riding---the Rodgers children even had their own pony.

Each summer, the Rodgers family would head to Ocean City, N.J., for a month.

"We'd cover ourselves with baby oil to get a tan," says Tina. "I never thought much about that until 45 years later, when I got melanoma."

Freckles, emblematic of her Irish heritage, covered Tina's face.

"My mother told us they were signs of beauty. What was she going to say?"

When it came time for high school, Tina took the entrance exam for Marywood Seminary, where her sister, Nancy Kay, then was a senior. A week later, the school's directress phoned to say that Tina had scored highest in the test and thus had won a full scholarship to the private high school.

"I actually laughed," recalls Tina. "I had left that test before it was over because I had a nosebleed. Must have been an easy test."

Tina suffered many nosebleeds as a child. She recalls that, when she was in eighth grade, she lay on the living room floor for at least six hours while Mary Sileo, the family's housekeeper, attended to her. Finally, the doctor came and cauterized Tina's nose.

"To this day, I have no idea what caused those nosebleeds. And God knows why we didn't go to the hospital."

Since she was 3, when doctors said she had a weak muscle in her left eye, Tina wore glasses.

"When I was 12, the doctor talked about an operation. My mother took me to another ophthalmologist and he said I didn't need glasses!"

***

Marywood Seminary, an all-girls' school, was located in the motherhouse of the IHM Sisters. As in grade school, Tina wore a uniform---actually, two uniforms because, in addition to the Marywood Seminary standard blue uniform with white shirt, the girls also had white pique dresses and jackets for special Masses in the school's ornate chapel.

Tina may have been a scholarship student, but the school got its money's worth from her mother.

"She was president of the Seminary Mothers' Club and put in a lot of time with the group's annual card party and other events. She also had been president of the Mothers' Club at Scranton Prep, the Jesuit school that my brothers Hugh J. and Michael attended. I think my mother, who had an associates degree from The Wharton School at Penn, was able to use her business acumen in her volunteer work."

The "Sem" education, in Tina's estimation, ranged from "okay" to "not for real." She and many of her friends believe that some nuns on the faculty were assigned there because the Mother Superior, who resided in the same building, wanted to keep an eye on them.

"For senior English, we had a nun who was in her 90s, I think, and she would walk up and down the room with her finger pointed at us. Believe me, I do not have the background in the classics that I should have."

Still, Tina enjoyed Marywood Seminary, where she captained the school's basketball team (in the two-dribbles-only era) and played on the field hockey squad. The latter had a perfect record for the four years during which Tina was a center halfback---the team lost every game.

For college, Tina chose Wheeling College, now Wheeling Jesuit University, in West Virginia, where she studied history. The college's small enrollment, she says, gave students a chance to spend time discussing issues with the Jesuit fathers, and thinking critically courtesy of the mandated minor in philosophy.

She often traveled to Wheeling on a private jet from a company owned by the family of a classmate, Mary Anne Fidati.

"Kindergarten by limousine and college by private plane," laughs Tina. "Not bad for a girl from Dunmore."

Before her senior year, Tina spent the summer as an intern at The Scranton Times, where she worked in the only editorial department open to women---the social pages. She was paid $50 a week, while the other intern---a male collegian working as a general assignment reporter---earned $80 a week.

Nevertheless, the Times experience convinced her that she should take a crack at a newspaper career. So she applied to a number of graduate journalism schools.

"I decided on the University of Missouri because it had such a great reputation."

***

Because she lacked a bachelor's degree in journalism, Tina was required to take a number of undergraduate prerequisites while she was struggling with graduate work at the "J School." A year later, the two Scranton papers came calling as each was seeking to hire another female staffer for its society pages. Tina had completed all requirements for her master's except for her thesis, so she headed home from Missouri and interviewed for both jobs; she took the higher-paying one at the Scrantonian-Tribune. She received her degree after completing her thesis.

Working in Scranton was a "kick," as Tina tells her students today. The small Tribune newsroom, replete with Remington typewriters, had a salt pill dispenser on the wall---"reporters took the pills when it was hot before the paper finally put in an air-conditioning unit. And they put that in backwards."

She and Gene Brislin started writing a column, "Noonbeams and Nightcaps," about the local social scene, and "everyone in town seemed interested in getting their names in it," Tina says.

The paper lacked a copy desk, so Tina edited her own work.

"Once I wrote about a 'new infant.' As if there were old ones. A copy editor surely would have helped."

These days, as she teaches ethics in her classes at William Paterson University, she always alludes to her days at The Tribune.

"Let's see---the reporter covering our Congressman was also paid to do PR for him. The editor of the television section handled PR for a local station. Conflict-of-interest meant nothing in those days. The publishers did not seem to care. And Christmas Eve was unbelievable---gifts were coming in for staffers all day long from politicians, owners of local companies---anyone who wanted good media coverage. I often thought it would make a good case study for modern media ethics textbooks."

Through a friend, Tina met John Lesher, an Army veteran who worked for IBM in Scranton. After they became engaged in 1969, John entered the MBA program at the Wharton School at the

University of Pennsylvania in Philadelphia. Tina later headed there to work on the copydesk of The Philadelphia Inquirer. They wed in August 1970 and lived in a tiny apartment at Washington Square near Independence Hall. A few months later, Tina's culinary foibles were evidenced as she tried to prepare the then-popular fondue. When the pot of oil exploded, she wound up with serious burns on her arms and legs.

"So much for my cooking," she says today as she eyes the scars.

For Tina, the copyediting position meant lots of nights and weekends on the job.

She had a chance to work with veteran editors whom, she says "taught me a lot," and to earn enough money to help support John through his graduate work.

                                    ***

When John took a job with Prudential's Real Estate Department in Newark, the Leshers moved to Elizabeth, N.J. Their daughter, Melissa, was born there---on the same day in 1972 that Tina's mother, who had passed away unexpectedly, was buried in Scranton.

"It was an unbelievable period of my life," says Tina. "People sent me congratulations and sympathy cards in the same envelope. And to think I missed my own mother's funeral..."

A transfer took the Leshers later that year to the Hartford area and Tina---out of boredom--- took a part-time evening job on the copydesk of The Hartford Courant.

"We were still in the pencil-and-paper mode at papers, although The Courant brought in a few computers for us to test in the back of the newsroom late at night."

Christian, the Leshers' second child (and second 10-pounder) was born in 1973 in Hartford. By the fall of 1974, as a result of another Prudential transfer, the Leshers had moved to Needham, a town near Boston; their third child, Brendan, was born in Massachusetts in early 1975.

Tina was head-first into motherhood---and free-lance writing for local papers. She had her first foray into writing a humor column and "loved it."

One of her columns focused on John's phone call to her to report that he had been transferred---again. Tina wrote that, before her spouse revealed where they would be heading, she guessed about "interesting" places they might be assigned: San Francisco? Denver? New Orleans?

Then John told her: Newark, N.J.

"I grabbed the phone book and looked up cardiologist," she wrote. "I figured I might as well call before I have a heart attack. Then I read John the riot act---hell, it probably was written in Newark."

The column won a lot of response from amused readers, but the Leshers still moved back to Jersey, this time to Westfield.

***

Writing and editing always have been Tina Lesher's bread-and-butter. Shortly after she returned to New Jersey in 1977, Tina began writing part-time as the religion writer and features writer at The Courier-News, a Gannett paper. Later, she wrote weekly food articles for The Elizabeth Daily Journal ("you don't have to cook to write," she argued when she accepted an award for her food writing), and also authored a humor column there. In addition, she moved into the public relations realm, handling publicity/PR for a number of local non-profits.

"Basically, I could stay home with the kids and use my writing or editing skills to continue my career," says Tina, who also took on corporate writing assignments.

In 1982, Tina heard that Seton Hall University was looking for a journalism instructor, so she applied and took the job. Three years later, at age 40, she became a fulltime doctoral student in English education at Rutgers. She immersed herself in her dissertation work---research into the writing coach movement in the American newsroom--- and traveled more than 10,000 miles to secure the data. In 1989, she joined the faculty at William Paterson. In her years there, she has served as chairman of the Communication Department, started a new college paper, and moved through the ranks to the full-professor level. Tina also spent two terms as president of the New Jersey Press Women. In 2001, she accepted a sabbatical appointment at Zayed University in the United Arab Emirates.

"That was one of the most interesting periods of my life," says Tina. "I taught for a semester at a university for national women in Abu Dhabi, a place that has changed in 40 years from a desert community to a thriving metropolis."

John's gift of a standup comedy class gave Tina the opportunity to appear twice at Caroline's Comedy Club on Broadway.

"I get material from my college classes. And I wish I really had done something like this ages ago. Some people actually think I am funny."

If she is passionate about teaching and writing, she also enjoys time on the golf course at Echo Lake Country Club in Westfield.

"I never seem to improve much, but I enjoy it," says Tina, noting that she and John, who now works in the real estate development field in Manhattan, love to travel and often play golf when they are away.

For 20 years, Tina has threatened to write a book about Club' 43 because, she says, "I think these women are so interesting."

The 60th birthday observances proved an impetus to get her going on the manuscript.

"I am the writer and the editor---same as usual."

Tina Lesher

In Dubai, UAE (2001)
Photo booth (1955)
50th Birthday Party with
Mary McEnerney (1993)
Monmouth Park
Race Track (2003)

HAPPY BIRTHDAY TINA LESHER
Purse - $16,000

Shire

Mary Clyne McEnerney

Today, the mention of New York's South Bronx conjures up images of ravaged buildings that resemble a war-torn area. But in the 1940s and 1950s, up around 140th Street in the South Bronx, "everybody had their doors open," says Mary McEnerney. "Everyone knew everyone else. People would stop by for a cup of tea."

It was here that Mary Clyne---now Mary McEnerney---lived in one of the apartment buildings that housed a lot of the immigrant Jewish, German and Irish families.

"We did not have many luxuries," says Mary. "My mother would save for a little vacation in Rockaway. We did not have a phone until I was in the fifth grade."

Today, "Mary Mac" is one of Westfield's most successful real estate brokers; now she carries a sophisticated cell phone to facilitate the listing and selling of homes with seven-figure tags.

As she thinks back to her life and friends in the South Bronx, though, Mary says matter-of-factly: "I didn't know I was poor; guess it was because I was surrounded by so many friends in the neighborhood."

***

Mary's mother, the former Alice McTeague, was born in 1901 and came to the United States right after the Depression to cook and serve as a housekeeper for a wealthy family.

"She never saw a black person until she got to New York," says Mary.

People were in such dire straits at the time that Alice would take the leftover food from her employer's kitchen and give it to the elevator men and others who worked in the area.

At age 39, she married another Irish immigrant, Michael Clyne. Alice was 42 when Mary was born; she gave birth to a son, Michael, four years later.

Mary's father worked at National City Bank as head of maintenance. Her mother toiled simultaneously as a housekeeper at the residences of Floyd Hall, chairman of the board of Eastern Airlines, and of Holland Farr, a Sloan-Kettering Hospital physician. Alice would come home at 3:30 or 4 p.m. after a long day of raising other families' children.

"Yet she fussed over everyone," says Mary. "She was that kind of person."

Mary remembers that her friends, Geri and Kathleen Kennedy, sisters who lived in another apartment in the building, got a television long before other families purchased sets. So Mary would go over to their home and watch "Howdy Doody" and "I Remember Mama."

They all went to St. Luke's, a Catholic grammar school staffed by nuns from the Dominican order.

"We walked to school and came home for lunch," Mary recalls. "A lot different from today…"

Mary and her friends continued their Catholic education after eighth grade, moving on to the Dominicans' Aquinas High, an all-girls' school. The girls used public buses to transport them to the school near Arthur Avenue in the Bronx. In addition to the strong academic curriculum, the Aquinas students were taught how to sew, a skill that would pay off for Mary in later years.

Her father took ill ("he was sick from about the time I was 11") and passed away when Mary was 16. While Alice thought about moving her two children out of the declining neighborhood, she couldn't afford to do so. For one thing, she didn't drive, and she needed to be near public transportation to continue her housekeeping jobs.

***

At the time of her father's death, Mary was contemplating becoming a nun.

"It was tough on my mother," Mary states. "But she was thrilled."

In those days, having a son or daughter enter the religious life was considered an honor for Catholic parents. So Alice accepted her daughter's decision with delight, and she helped Mary buy what she needed to enter the convent.

As Mary looks back today on her decision to leave her widowed mother and head to the convent, she states frankly: "I think I was selfish."

She chose the Dominican Order in Blauvelt, N.Y; the nuns are affiliated with the Dominican Order in Adrian, Mich., where fellow Club '43 member Cathy Farrell Rock entered the convent the same year. But whereas the Adrian segment is under the direct jurisdiction of the Pope, the Blauvelt nuns report to the Archdiocese of New York.

Mary had a great-aunt who was a Blauvelt Dominican. In fact, there were a lot of "religious" in the family.

"They were so poor they became 'religious,'" Mary contends.

Moving into the motherhouse in Blauvelt in Rockland County proved "tough---very tough" for Mary.

"It was country to me....surrounded by hills."

She was lonely as a postulant. She could not get phone calls. Letters were distributed once a week.

"We were not allowed to talk," she says. "We used sign language."

Thirty-two young women entered the teaching order in 1961; about half remain as of 2006 and Mary still meets with the group regularly.

***

For her first four years as a nun, Mary---who became Sister Alice Michael after her parents' names---attended Dominican College of Blauvelt for an education degree; her classmates were other sisters as well as lay students. When Alice could, she traveled to Rockland County to visit her daughter, who was not allowed to come home; it was several years later, in fact, before Mary could join her mother at home for Christmas Day.

Mary's first assignment as a nun was to teach second grade at St. Philip and James School in the Bronx. She spent four years there, working under the tutelage of Sister Corona Marie, a "marvelous principal," about whom Mary still raves.

"But we never watched TV and really couldn't talk to people," says Mary, noting that her mother got to visit her periodically at the school's convent. In addition to teaching, Sister Alice Michael was in charge of the chapel and the priests' vestments. She cleaned the floor on her knees and pressed the altar linens. Today Mary looks back at that time of her life, shakes her head and laughs: "My own kids never knew what an iron was."

***

The nuns at St. Philip and James had a car, and Mary secured her driver's license.

"I was always a little nervous about driving," she says. "Where was I going to drive? You mostly used public transportation then."

As for money, Mary had none: "I didn't need it."

Boosted by the liberal changes brought by the Vatican Council several years before, many nuns changed their habits (outfits) from the formal, stiff dress to shorter, suit-like garb. Mary was the first at her school to have the more modern outfit because she made it herself; after all, she stresses, "I learned to sew back in high school."

Even with all its restrictions, a nun's life in the 1960s was not as difficult in some respects as it may seem by today's standards, contends Mary.

"It is harder today, in a way. Years ago, when you got to be 60 and you were a nun, you did not have to worry about retirement."

Traditionally, younger nuns helped the elderly in their retirement years. But now, as Mary notes, "there is not another generation of nuns. So the orders are selling off their assets to fund retirement. It is sad, in a way."

Mary's life as a nun did not remove her from concerns about her family. She was happy that her brother did not have to serve in the Vietnam conflict---he was waived because he was the lone son of a widowed mother---but she was worried about her mother remaining in her Bronx neighborhood. With some prodding from her daughter-nun, Alice moved in 1967 to an apartment in St. Nicholas of Tolentine parish near Fordham University in the Bronx.

For Mary, the hardest part of her religious life came when she decided to leave the convent. She made the decision more than a year before she parted ways with the Dominicans in June 1969.

"To leave the convent---it is like splitting up. I knew it was embarrassing for my mother," who was told of Mary's plans about six months before the actual departure date.

"And to tell Sister Corona Marie...aye, aye, aye," says Mary.

***

One thing Mary knew: she did not want to teach after her she got out because, she chuckles, "it is not a great place to meet men."

She moved to the corporate world, in a job at Eastern Airlines where she was in charge of organizing sales representatives' seminars. The firm had a hiring freeze at the time, and her coworkers figured "that somebody knew somebody at 10 Rockefeller Plaza," says Mary.

True. It was Mary's mother, Alice, who certainly knew someone—the airline's chairman, for whom she still worked as a housekeeper. Alice also had connections to get Mary the right clothes for her first out-of-the-religious-life job. Mrs. Farr, the physician's wife for whom Alice worked in her other housekeeping job, took Mary to the "consignment place" at Sloan-Kettering Hospital in New York. The shop was not open to the public at the time, but Mary was able to secure the appropriate corporate wardrobe at consignment prices.

Eastern proved a "great" place to work for Mary, who traveled extensively in her post.

"After four months out of the convent, I was in Vienna. I went to Hawaii. All my friends who had never been nuns hated me...they were jealous. The job---it was a whole different world for me after eight years as a nun."

***

While living at home with Alice, Mary adopted a typical social life of the times---down to the Jersey shore with friends in the summer and then a share in a Hunter Mountain ski house in winter. It was there that she met fellow New Yorker John McEnerney right before New Years 1970 and started dating him. The following spring, Eastern Airlines moved out of Manhattan to Miami and she was offered a transfer there.

"I didn't want to refuse, but I didn't want to move there," says Mary, who returned to the teaching fold. This time it was at a public school in Yonkers, N.Y., where she" hated" her assignment: teaching fifth grade. Soon her life was getting too busy---she was starting her master's at Fordham, commuting (with a fellow teacher who had a car) to Yonkers every day and preparing for her wedding to John. So she opted for a new job---teaching second grade, as she did when she was a nun---at St. Nicholas of Tolentine School, just two blocks away from home. It was at the parish church there where John and Mary exchanged wedding vows in 1971.

They initially lived in the Bronx before deciding to follow John's brother, Peter, and his wife, Ronnie, who had moved to Westfield. Mary was pregnant when she and John settled in nearby Fanwood, N.J. But after just a few weeks, tragedy struck. In her sixth month of pregnancy, Mary delivered and lost twins. She remembers their coffins and their local burial and says: 'It was very sad."

Mary took a stab at substitute teaching but found it hard with driving to districts not close to Fanwood. Her life changed, though, she says, when she met a woman named Carol Wood who convinced Mary to make a move into real estate sales.

"And," in Mary's own words, "the rest is history."

***

For more than three decades, Mary Mac has made her mark in Westfield area real estate with overall sales close to the $300 million mark. She claims that her background as a teacher has helped with her work.

"Ex-teachers and nurses do well in real estate," she says. "They are used to nurturing," an important commodity in dealing with buyers and sellers.

Things have changed over the decades in the real estate field, Mary notes.

"Today it is so time-consuming. Years ago, you saw a house, liked it and they gave you a mortgage. Today, so many places give mortgages and you need pre-approvals, inspections and all that."

Working in the real estate field translates to a "social atmosphere," Mary claims. "I have made so many friends in the past 30 years and I keep in touch with them. Many of my wonderful customers have become very dear friends."

Mary's foray into the working world was eased when her mother retired in her mid-70s and moved out of The Bronx and into Mary's home to help with the children. (The McEnerneys have two daughters, Allison and Tara, both now married). Alice lived into her 90th year.

"She sacrificed all her life," says a grateful Mary. "She had to commute. She worked her entire life. She never complained. What I do is so easy compared to what my mother did."

***

In Fall 1999, Mary began to feel ill. She went to several physicians to find out why she was not sleeping and why her ankles were swelling.

"I was feeling light-headed when I was driving," she explains.

The tests came back negative. Then one day in late November, Mary had an appointment with her gynecologist, Alice Gibbons, for a routine check-up. After listening to Mary describe her problems, the doctor picked up the phone and called an affiliated cardiology group to describe Mary's symptoms.

Dr. Gibbons then looked at Mary and said: "You are going into congestive heart failure." Within an hour, Mary was admitted to Overlook Hospital in Summit. She shakes her head to this day as she recalls what a cardiologist there said to her: "What does a woman gynecologist know abut cardiology?"

The gynecologist's intervention actually proved life-saving. When hospital doctors put a monitor on Mary, they discovered the seriousness of the situation. Mary was moved to coronary intensive care; the next day, she got a pacemaker.

A month later, Mary was hospitalized for a blood clot on the heart. She continues to take medication to this day to deal with that problem.

One thing she learned from the experience, though: "You must be an advocate for your own health."

***

Her years as a nun have played an important part of Mary's character.

"I benefited from life as a nun. I got my education. I may never have finished college. I met some phenomenal people, like Sister Corona Marie, who is now in her 90s. I was really blessed to be in that environment."

Today, Mary McEnerney carries a date-filled calendar around as she moves from appointment to appointment in her high-powered career,

"I'm like an old nun," Mary says as she makes a notation in her book. "I like seeing everything in front of me."

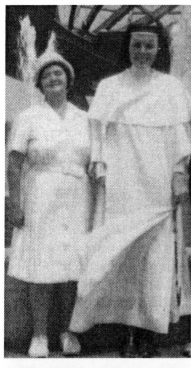

Mary McEnerney

Sister Alice Michael
  with her mother (1966)
With Sister Corona Marie (2004)
Sister Alice Michael
  with her class (1967)

Diana Geer McGonigle

While Diana Geer McGonigle was completing her bachelor's degree at the University of Pennsylvania in the late 1960s, she took a part-time job at Philadelphia General Hospital. Diana already was a registered nurse and proudly wore the cap of St. Luke's Hospital School of Nursing, Bethlehem, Pa., where she was graduated a few years earlier.

At the time, capping ceremonies were an integral part of nursing school activities.

Donning that important cap proved a milestone for nurses. A patient or hospital visitor easily could recognize the rank of a nurse---RN or LPN---from the cap bearing the wearer's alma mater

One day, Diana arrived at Philadelphia General for her shift, but she had forgotten to bring along her cap. As she began her rounds to deliver medications, another nurse handed Diana a cap.

"So I plopped a Philadelphia General cap on my head and started out to deliver the medications to patients."

Diana was in the midst of her assignment when someone came up to her and said the director of nursing wanted to see her.

"I was annoyed," says Diana. "I wanted to finish giving medications."

She walked down the hall and into the office of the director, who grabbed the cap and said: "what do you think you're doing by impersonating a Philadelphia General nurse?"

Diana explained that she had forgotten her nursing cap and had borrowed the Philadelphia General one.

The director did not care. She told Diana, "you are out of here. Get your final check."

Admittedly upset, Diana went to her apartment and called her then-boyfriend, a neurology resident at the hospital. He told her to sit tight and he would look into it because he had heard from other doctors that the director was "doing things like this."

Three days later, while Diana was talking to her mother on the phone, an operator cut in with a call from the nursing director.

"Miss Geer," she said, "I think there were hasty things said. You should come back."

Diana had the presence of mind to say simply: "I will think about it."

It turned out that the director was a political appointee already under fire for some questionable actions. She was reassigned shortly thereafter to a nursing home post.

As for Diana, she felt "ill at ease" about the incident and soon left the hospital's employ.

Still, the experience shows the importance of nursing caps in the profession's history. The wearing of nursing caps went by the wayside in the 1980s for a variety of reasons, including the argument that they were not hygienic.

***

Diana Geer was about 13 when she and her mother moved from Connecticut to Bethlehem, Pa, and into the home of Diana's aunt, a widow with five children.

"My parents divorced--- I assume they got divorced; actually, my mother never talks about it," says Diana.

The move was "traumatic" for Diana, who went from "being an only child into a home with five cousins."

She had a "terrible" relationship" with her father, she says, claiming he was an alcoholic who could not hold a job. And, she says candidly, "once, he tried to---well--- kidnap me!"

It was just a few weeks after Diana had moved to her aunt's home when a commotion erupted in the middle of the night.

"Stay where you are," yelled Diana's relatives to her.

Her father had broken into the home along with the dog that Diana left behind in Connecticut. Her aunt called the police, who hauled Diana's father away to jail.

"He said he wanted to bring me the dog. But he really wanted me," says Diana. "He was incensed that my mother would take me away."

Released from jail a few days later, Diana's father left Bethlehem with the dog.

Diana had no correspondence from her father from that day forward.

"No birthday cards---nothing," she says.

The next time Diana saw her father was years later. She was just out of nursing school and wanted to satisfy her curiosity about the man. So she drove to Virginia, to a trailer where he lived.

"We were kind of like strangers," she states.

She never saw him again; he died when Diana was about 31.

***

For Diana, high school in Bethlehem was an "innocent time." She "loved" the Friday night dances and fondly remembers the jitterbug, emblematic of the rock 'n roll dancing that marked the era.

Diana always felt that she did not have as much as others--- no siblings, one parent, etc. She and her mother had moved to an apartment, while her high school friends lived in homes with two parents.

"I felt short-changed," Diana says 40-plus years later.

Yet she stresses her strong admiration for her mother, now in her 90s and relatively independent until her recent move to Diana's Westfield home. "She is the closest person I have."

Diana's mom, Elsie Grein Geer, was reared in Dansville, a town in upstate New York. She started working right after high school when she boarded a train, with a trunk in tow, to work for Western Union as a substitute teletype operator. Her assignments would stretch for about two weeks at a time at train stations or hotels throughout upstate New York.

Elsie would ship home her trunk regularly with her laundry. One time, her mother---Diana's maternal grandmother--- decided to put some peaches in the return laundry shipment.

"The peaches smashed and ruined all the clothes," says Diana as she smilingly relates the story told by Elsie.

Elsie, who really wished she could have been a teacher, moved on to a secretarial job in Virginia after her marriage to Diana's father, who was in the Navy when the family lived in the Old Dominion state. When Diana and her mother came to Bethlehem, the latter went to work in printing at Bethlehem Steel, the mainstay of the city's economy. There she eventually worked with computers and retired when she was 62. She later traveled extensively and continued to win awards for volunteerism.

"She was working with Meals on Wheels at the seniors' housing," laughs her daughter. "She was in her 90s and delivering meals to seniors!"

***

Diana's late uncle, a physician, had left a scholarship at St. Luke's Hospital School of Nursing in Bethlehem. Her aunt, a nurse, encouraged Diana to go to nursing school, a haven for many young women in the 1960s and before. The three-year diploma schools, so prevalent at the time, since have given way to nursing programs that lead to baccalaureate degrees.

For Diana, St. Luke's nursing school, like others of that era, was "very restrictive. But you were cared for. Lights out by 10 o'clock. You felt safe."

In Diana's estimation, the instructors were "ancient.

"They were probably 40, but looked 60 and acted 80. They hated my teased hair. They would measure our uniforms---had to be 13 inches to the ground."

Nursing students worked hard, completing shifts at the affiliated hospital.

"They really depended on us," states Diana.

Lehigh College, then an all-male institution, attracted top-notch students to its Bethlehem campus. The school's fraternity houses lined Delaware Avenue, where St. Luke's Nursing School was located. Consequently, Diana said she and her fellow nursing students "had a ball," even though housemothers checked out students' dates and men were not allowed past the living room.

After her graduation in 1964, Diana worked for a year at the hospital and took classes at nearby Moravian College. With few bachelor's in nursing programs available in the country, the government began to offer help to boost the professionalism of nurses. So Diana applied and received a federal traineeship that took her to the University of Pennsylvania to pursue her BSN degree; her award included full tuition plus a stipend for living expenses.

The Vietnam War was in full swing, but it "didn't really affect me," Diana contends. She admits her leanings were anti-war but, like many of her Club '43 members, the Vietnam protests were not a major part of her life.

***

After completing her UPenn studies, Diana took a position at the university's Pathology Department, where she worked with veterinarians on melanoma research. It was around this time that she met a young Exxon employee, Dan McGonigle, an alumnus of Penn's Wharton School of Business.

Meeting Dan "changed my life," says Diana.

After the pair wed and were living in the Philadelphia area, Diana decided that she wanted to teach nursing. But the day she secured a job in the educational sector was the same day her spouse came home to report he had been transferred to New York City. So the McGonigles moved to The Big Apple and Diana took a job at a doctor's office in Manhattan. She quit working after she had children---daughters Regan and Joanna. The family since has lived in Connecticut, Texas, and New Jersey; they also spent five years in Brussels, Belgium.

During the years overseas, the McGonigles traveled "everywhere," says Diana, as she and Dan tried to ground their offspring in the varied sights and cultures outside of Westfield and America. On a trip to a Masai village in Kenya, Diana remembers being told to bring presents---they brought toothbrushes.

"These trips made us appreciate what we have," says Diana.

Travel remains an important commodity for the McGonigles to this day. For their 60th birthdays---Dan also was born in 1943---the couple and their daughters celebrated by returning to Europe for a bicycle tour that included the Brussels area where they had lived when the girls were in grade school.

***

Until recently, Diana worked at a dermatologist's office in Westfield. She chuckles as she compares today's concerns relative to skin care to that when she was a nursing student.

"Then we just talked about psoriasis."

The biggest change she has witnessed over the decades is in the area of cosmetic dermatology. People want to look younger and many turn to the popular laser treatments. She has seen patients, about the ages of her daughters, who spend $500 for a BOTOX treatment that Diana sarcastically says "lasts for a few minutes." She does admit that, unlike in her younger days when she never went to a dermatologist, she sees a heightened concern from people about the need to watch their skin in light of the rising numbers of skin cancers.

Diana is one of the Club '43 officers in the ranks of breast cancer survivors.

At age 55, she was diagnosed with the disease and had a lumpectomy followed by radiation. She never told her mother about it until treatment was finished.

"I was devastated for awhile," says Diana. "It turned out to be treatable and everything is fine."

***

Diana McGonigle's quiet demeanor belies her strong support for women's rights. She has been a subscriber to MS magazine since its initial publication and she berates any attempt to treat women other than as equals. She bristles as she relates her nursing school experience where Diana and her classmates were told that "if a doctor comes in, you stand and give him your seat." She has made sure Regan and Joanna know not to bend to that type of subservient role in their careers.

Life at 60-plus for Diana is not like it was for the previous generations.

"I can picture my (maternal) grandmother with hair in a bun and dowdy shoes. She would just sit around...I never really saw her walk much. I could not even have a conversation with her."

It is quite the opposite for the active Diana, who in her early 60s remains active--- she still plays tennis and enjoys the world of travel.

"It really is a different life," she says.

Diana McGonigle

Nursing student (1963)
Cowgirl (1949)
With mother (2005)
Biking in France on 60th birthday
trip with family (2003)

Lesley Posner Robins

"We went like lambs to the slaughter."

That's Lesley Posner Robins' description of how she and her all-female freshman classmates at Vassar College in 1961 accepted the requirement of posing for photos in their Fundamentals of Movement class.

"These were NUDE photos," she exclaims.

The class, commonly known as "Fundies" by the Vassar girls, provided the young women with lessons on such topics as how to get a suitcase down from the overhead racks on the train and how to carry a tray.

"The grade," Lesley says, "was based on your carriage – how you carried yourself."

The students were told that one's posture was important, and the before and after photos would show how each student had progressed in that respect.

So the students posed – at the beginning of the course and again at the end.

Upper classmen advised the freshmen to slouch for the first photo so the later one would show an improvement in posture.

And, says Lesley, the older students also said to "tell them you have your period and you need to wear panties."

The Nude Posture Photos, as they became known decades later, were taken in the 1940s through the 1960s at Vassar and other top schools, including Smith, Mt. Holyoke, and Princeton. In 1992, George Hersey wrote in The New York Times that the photos had nothing to do with posture, but were taken as part of anthropological research to demonstrate that intelligence, worth and future achievement of the subjects at these elite schools could be predicted based on body type. The photos became the subject three years later of a New York Times Magazine cover story.

Vassar reportedly burned most of the photos by the 1970s.

But the nude posture photos still burn in Lesley's memories.

Expressing her dismay at "how naïve we were," Lesley claims, "we never asked questions. We never mentioned it to our parents. No one said a word."

***

Lesley grew up in what could be called a grand apartment house in Brooklyn.

Yet she has no perception really "of growing up in Brooklyn" in the 50s; she had no concept of a neighborhood.

"My father drove me to school. There were no kids in the building except a cousin."

She and her sister, Amy, were not even allowed to go trick-or-treating on Halloween.

"My father did not want us to bother people who had no kids living with them anymore."

Her parents were a well-educated couple. Shirley Posner had taught school for a brief period; Dr. Leonard Posner was a practicing ophthalmologist.

The couple spoke English and Yiddish at home, and used the latter "when they didn't want us to know what they were saying," recalls Lesley. "Thus they had a language for 'secret' communications."

Unlike today with families scattered all over the country, Lesley had her maternal grandparents living only a few buildings away. She often visited them after school, and they were a very important part of her extended family.

For Lesley, grade school was an experience shared by relatively few.

She attended the "progressive" Brooklyn Community School, modeled on the principles of John Dewey, who was considered one of the most influential thinkers of his day on education. Dewey backed experiential-supported experimental education wherein pupils engaged in hands-on activities that demanded thinking, which would result in learning.

"One of my teachers had been blackballed in the McCarthy investigations," says Lesley, alluding to the famed 1950s hearings led by U.S. Sen. Joseph McCarthy to root out Communist subversives.

Singer Pete Seeger, who was cited for contempt by the House on Un-American Activities Committee after refusing to name members of left-wing groups to which he belonged, was godfather to a teacher's child.

"We were such champions for Seeger," says Lesley, explaining that the school "had everything to do with freedom of speech."

At Brooklyn Community School, Lesley and her schoolmates called teachers by their first names. The classes were small -- about 15 in each -- but a student was not in the typical seventh or eighth grade.

"Grades were named by our ages; we had all started in the threes," smiles Lesley. "Rather than being in the eighth grade when we graduated, we were in the 13s."

She and her fellow students were aware of what a card-carrying Communist was, says Lesley.

"I knew it was bad, but I did not know why it was bad."

She finds it interesting that, although they sent her to a progressive school, her parents never talked about Ethel and Julius Rosenberg, the couple executed in 1953 for conspiracy to commit espionage.

And, like their parents when they were growing up, Lesley and Amy exited New York in the summer to attend camp in Massachusetts. The all-girls' Camp Romaca was located in the Berkshires, nearby the home the Posners bought years later and still own. Life at camp in the 1950s was "idealistic and very loving" for Lesley. Years later, at camp reunions, she was amazed to hear the counselors talk about being lesbians.

"Unbelievable," says Lesley. "We were so naïve; we had no idea."

***

Given a choice by her parents to attend a private or a public high school, Lesley picked the latter. She wanted a big school--- not the one closest in proximity to her home --- and with the help of a family friend who headed the English Department at Midwood High School in Brooklyn, she and her sister were able to get in there.

Like many growing up in the 50s, Lesley began piano lessons early in life, but in her own estimation, "I was not good." She gravitated to the flute and became active in Midwood's Marching Band.

Lesley also attended Sunday School at Union Temple, a part of the big Reform Movement breaking off from Orthodox Judaism. Since the services and schooling were in English, Lesley was not required to learn Hebrew "and feels bad about that" to this day. She was confirmed but, unlike many of her friends who belonged to Conservative temples, she had no Bat Mitzvah, the ceremonial occasion when a young person is recognized as an adult in the Jewish faith. Today, Lesley belongs to Westfield's active Temple Emanu-El, which she describes as "Reform, leaning to Conservative."

***

In the fall of 1961, the year that Vassar College marked its centennial, Lesley Posner entered Vassar. The initial convocation for students took place in the institution's chapel and Lesley was in "awe" of the structure.

"It was so gorgeous. The building is to die for."

What she clearly remembers about the program were the words directed at the new students from Vassar's then-president, Sarah Gibson Blanding.

"She said 'you are intelligent women. These four years are for concentration on your minds. This education is not about your body, but about your intellect.'"

From her seat in the assemblage, Lesley was shocked.

"In essence, the president was saying to us that we were not to think about having sex. I was shocked that she would say that in public. I couldn't believe anyone would want sex anyway. It all blew me away."

The 60s have enjoyed a reputation as a decade of protests, but Lesley never saw them.

"The 60s were not tumultuous for me. I got MS Magazine and got mad as hell at times, but I was not doing anything like protesting."

Lesley's own experiences provide a look into how dating patterns differed a generation ago. Students at all-girls' colleges often were invited to spend weekends visiting their dates at all-male institutions.

"We would go with someone we hardly knew," she says.

When she was a junior, she was invited to Princeton by one of these young men. By the time they made it to Sunday brunch, Lesley was "sick of this guy." She started talking to another student, Martin Robins, a rabid New York Mets fan, about the new Shea Stadium.

"I never introduced myself to him, though," says Lesley.

Martin somehow got hold of a Vassar Freshman Faces book for the college's Class of '65 and picked out her picture. Actually, it was another girl's photo; coincidentally, she had been a high school friend of Lesley's and sat next to her in a philosophy class and knew that Lesley had been at Princeton for the weekend. When Lesley's friend was contacted by Martin, she was able to get the message to the right person -- Lesley. Shortly thereafter, Lesley received a letter from Martin.

"So I wrote him back," says Lesley, stressing that, in those days, "it was inappropriate for a girl to call a boy!"

Martin then phoned her to set up a date at Vassar.

"I was so excited that, as I hung up the phone, I yelled 'Yeah.'"

She never imagined that Martin could hear those loud words of excitement. After they were married, though, he informed her that he heard the screaming and "knew he was in" with Lesley.

Martin, who eventually would rise to executive posts in the New Jersey/New York transportation industry, also is a Brooklyn native; ironically, he had his tonsils removed in a doctor's office in the apartment building where the Posners resided. But when he was young, he moved with his family to Linden, N. J, where he spent most of his growing-up years.

"He had different experiences than I did," his wife argues. "He grew up in a neighborhood."

When Lesley and the rest of the Class of 1965 finished Vassar, their careers -- like most women coming out of most colleges those days -- ventured into one of two areas: either they became teachers or nurses. Many headed straight to wedded bliss.

Lesley got married right out of college and moved with Martin to Cambridge, MA., where he was a Harvard Law School student and she took a post as a junior high school English teacher in nearby Acton.

***

By 1972, when Lesley and Martin were residing in Westfield with their three preschool-aged sons (twins Todd and Drew, and James), she began part-time classes in pursuit of a master's degree at Kean College. She chose to study in a reading specialization program.

"When I was in Acton, there were 15 and 16-year-olds in remedial class; I thought they were demeaned. So I decided to study reading and work with older kids." After receiving her degree three years later, Lesley started teaching Reading and Study Skills part-time at Union County College. There she began to understand that a lot of what she taught was connected to writing, but that the pieces of the English curriculum were unconnected. So she decided to pursue a program in writing -- also at Kean -- with the objective of teaching adult students to write.

Since then, writing instruction has been an integral part of Lesley's professional repertoire. After a lawyer-friend showed her "hideous" writing by an attorney, she joined a firm dedicated to teaching lawyers how to improve their writing skills. By 1984, she was on her own with Lesley Robins Associates, instructing a clientele that included engineers as well as lawyers. At one point she hired a few employees.

"The way I conduct my business is very one-on-one, very personal. Ultimately, I preferred to have fewer clients at one time and give them all very attentive service than have employees who rarely could give the kind of service I did."

Lesley continues to this day as a well-recognized writing consultant with a cadre of clients in northern New Jersey and New York.

***

In 1998, at age 55, Lesley Robins "felt a lump" on her breast. The timing was bad -- her youngest son was to be married shortly in California so Lesley kept quiet about the discovery until after the ceremonies.

"As soon as I got home, the madness began. I got all the tests and the surgeon said: 'We will do a lumpectomy so that we can have a highly accurate biopsy. It's outpatient surgery.' I never had surgery in my life, and the day of the lumpectomy I was terrified. I was shaking. I remember being on a gurney afterwards and can still hear the surgeon say 'It's malignant.' I didn't believe it. I felt like I was in a dream. That night my son and his wife were coming to New Jersey on their way home from their honeymoon. I couldn't talk, so we just all sat and cried. My sister flew down from Cambridge. We cried."

Her mother, then 79, had just lost her last sibling. When Shirley Posner found out about her daughter's cancer, she was "horrified." But she and other family members rallied as a support network when the cancer news broke.

Further surgery was performed to remove more tissue and lymph nodes.

"They found some cancer in two lymph nodes," says Lesley. "The good news was that it was only in the first two of 14."

Chemotherapy and radiation followed; Martin came for every treatment.

Lesley did not "crash" until the treatments were over.

"Then I was a wreck. It was the worst year of my life."

Lesley sought out a support group and found one through St. Barnabas Hospital in Livingston. N.J. Still, she had trouble putting her life back together.

"I couldn't read for two years -- nothing. I did not teach, but I continued with my writing work for two of my clients, which was a 'godsend.'"

As she thinks about that period of her life, though, she says candidly: "when you are in the middle of breast cancer, it's like being in a black hole, and you don't think you'll ever get out of it."

***

Today, Lesley Posner Robins ponders the generational differences from an interesting perspective.

As a mother and grandmother, she can see how different the next generations are. As a woman over 60, she still has parents and their vitality amazes her ("my mother still plays golf and my father is into computers").

Her own generation---and that of her fellow Club '43 members---is a special group, in Lesley's estimation.

"Our generation has benefited from having a foot in the old---and in the new. It is really something."

Lesley Robins

One year old with mother
  (1944)
With sons at camp
  (1980)
Four generations
  (2005)

LINNEA WEIS RHODES

When Club '43 members were young, the concept of day care was not an acceptable option for most American families. Dr. Benjamin Spock, the heralded pediatrician, noted in books published in 1947 and 1958 that it made no sense for mothers to pay other people to do a poorer job of bringing up children.

By the time Club '43 members were raising their own children, though, day care had become an accepted reality in communities, even where two-earner families were prevalent---and Westfield was no exception. Westfield Day Care Center (WDCC) had become an important cog in the town's child-rearing arena.

In the late 1980s, Linnea Weis Rhodes, a homemaker who had been active in many town organizations, traveled one day to Manhattan to see a play with her theatre group friends. One of them, Janet Burchett, a board member at WDCC, told Linnea that the center was seeking a part-time bookkeeper. She wanted Linnea to take the job.

Linnea's experience?

She had handled the treasurer's jobs for a few parent-teacher organizations in town.

"No one ever wanted to do it, so I always wound up being the treasurer," says Linnea. "I learned how to balance the books."

With her sons at an age when they would be heading for college soon, Linnea took on the WDCC bookkeeping duties.

"Little by little, I kept doing more."

In a brief period, the WDCC director resigned and her replacement did not last long. At that point, Linnea was asked to be the interim director of the center until a permanent director joined the staff.

"I didn't want the fulltime job," says Linnea, who nevertheless agreed to help out temporarily.

As she immersed herself into the new responsibilities, she began to attend conferences and become more involved in the administrative and other aspects of day care work.

"I loved it," she admits.

As a result, she spent 10 years as the highly-regarded director of the Westfield Day Care Center before she retired to "travel, play golf and enjoy life."

***

Babysitters or daycare were out of the question, though, in the 1940s and 50s for Linnea Weis and her brother, Stephen, who is two years older. When Linnea was 5, the family moved from Maplewood, N.J., to nearby Springfield. Her mother, Dorothy, worked---"my parents needed the money," says Linnea---at a relative's heating contracting firm in Madison, and relied on public transportation to make the commute.

"We were on our own for an hour after school," says Linnea. "There wasn't a babysitter."

If Dorothy Weis arrived home a bit later than usual because of train or bus problems, her children would start to misbehave and their yelling would increase in volume.

"She was madder as she got closer," recalls Linnea about her mother's view of the kids' embarrassing behavior.

Linnea's parents, both of German descent, grew up in three-family homes; relatives lived in the other apartments and the buildings next door. When it was time for dinner, they all often headed to the family having the most interesting offering that night.

By the time she was 10, Linnea had moved with her family back to her father's native Maplewood where she spent time with a flock of cousins from her own generation.

Her father, Paul, worked in the orders department of the New York based S. H. Kress and Company until he lost his job in the mid-50s; he then began working at a Millburn hardware store, close to Maplewood. Linnea's mother later traded her commuting job for a post in the tax office at Maplewood's Town Hall.

Life in Maplewood was much like that in other New Jersey suburban towns.

In winter, the pond at the town park was flooded so youngsters could skate at night and sit around a campfire. In the good weather, Linnea and her friends learned to play tennis at private lessons at Maplewood Country Club.

Unlike those in the next generation, the youngsters of the period were "independent," in Linnea's estimation.

"No one was looking out for us. We could handle things."

In junior high, for example, she played in a girls' basketball league.

"No parents were involved like today in Westfield," she remarks. "The girls ran it themselves."

When a section of the junior high school was destroyed, reportedly at the hand of young arsonists, a group of students organized a fundraiser on their own.

"Our message," Linnea says, "was that we were the good kids; the bad kids burned down the school."

***

To Linnea Rhodes, aspirin is a "miracle drug."

That's probably because, as a child, she did not see a doctor nor take any medicine.

"I'm actually a third-generation Christian Scientist," she explains, noting that most of her current friends probably "would never believe it."

Her maternal grandmother, a Christian Science nurse, helped when others of the faith fell sick. But, when a relative died, Linnea says, "no one really knew what the person died of!"

Her parents began to draw away from Christian Science, but still would drive Linnea and Stephen to its local Sunday School every week.

"They would drop us off and keep driving," Linnea recalls.

As the years passed, Paul and Dorothy Weis began to give medicine to their offspring. By the time Linnea entered college, she had no part of Christian Science---"I thought it was crazy. My friends and I would joke about it."

Today, she smilingly embraces medicine and, she stresses: "I always get my annual checkups."

***

Linnea's artistic bent was evidenced from the time she was young. She no doubt inherited the talent from her mother, who was forced to give up a full scholarship to art school because she lacked support from her divorcing parents.

For Linnea, "art was a favorite subject."

Advanced art programs were not part of the curriculum in the South Orange-Maplewood schools at the time, but Linnea credits her art teachers for allowing her to learn from them. During her junior high and high school days, Linnea worked a few afternoons a week at the town library, where she enthusiastically lent her artistic ability to whatever project needed it.

Art proved to be her niche in life.

"I think in a family, you find that niche," muses Linnea. "I was different from my brother."

Stephen, a Merit Scholar, got a "full ride" to Cornell on a ROTC scholarship. After a year, he no longer wanted the Army-related training. So, with the family then funding his costs, Linnea's undergraduate options were, as she says, "local.

"I didn't question it. My academics were so-so anyway. And I really wanted to go to Douglass."

Douglass is the well-regarded women's college at Rutgers, the state university in New Brunswick, about a half-hour away from Maplewood. Linnea, to this day considered a good athlete, played on the Douglass softball, field hockey and tennis teams. As an art major, she specialized in graphics—etching, lithography, etc.

"I liked line drawings and I didn't have a strong background in color so I went into etching."

In that art form, being used for more than 500 years, the artist covers a blank metal plate with wax ground; then, with a special utensil, she draws a picture through the wax onto the metal. After an acid bath, the wax is removed and the cleaned plate has an image etched into it.

"You can't change it," explains Linnea. "It was the immediacy to it that appealed to me."

Her etchings depicted the lovely Victorian homes that line streets near Rutgers, as well as some of the university's imposing buildings. Today, scores of the etchings she created in college remain in her Westfield home.

Her etching talent is displayed elsewhere, too. In the 1990s, Linnea visited a retired Douglass dean at her home in Troy, N.Y. She was surprised—and delighted---to see one of her etchings framed and displayed in the home.

***

When it came time to secure a job after college graduation in 1961, Linnea found the prospects for a fine art major to be limiting. She even applied to an encyclopedia company to write informational blurbs, but decided work like that "was boring." She settled at Norcross Greeting Cards, but not in a dream job.

"The message seemed to be that 'we don't like your art so we won't hire you as an artist' so I became assistant to the director of art," says Linnea, whose job was to help take art and turn it into cards.

"They never let me near the real art in my four years there," she laughs.

Living in Manhattan in the early 60s was "great" for Linnea and her friends. With no money, she first lived with two others in a Greenwich Village apartment. A year later, Linnea moved to her own studio apartment in the Chelsea section. She didn't live alone for long, though.

Linnea saw an ad that said: "Are You Lonely---Free Cats." She responded---and found herself in some lady's "filthy" apartment.

"There must have been 60 cats. Every horizontal space had a cat. You knew she must have been stealing these cats. Today this lady would be in the news."

Linnea wanted one of the felines, but the Cat Woman (as nicknamed by Linnea) told her to take two, so one was not lonely. For her free cats, Linnea had to buy a cat-carrying case from Cat Woman. Then it was off to the studio apartment with two new four-legged residents.

New York, with its cosmopolitan features, translated to a "wonderful place to live" for Linnea. She loved joining friends for a dinner out or a ride across the bridges on rented bikes. When the Beatles performed at Shea Stadium in 1966, Linnea and her friends were among the noisy fans in attendance.

Going out at all hours did not bother her.

"One night I was going to a friend's home late at night and I got in a taxi. I got a lecture from the cab driver about being out alone at that hour."

Vietnam was heating up but the war was not a major consideration for Linnea. Her best friend's husband went to the Southeast Asia conflict, and that raised some concern. Overall, though, the Vietnam War "was on the periphery of my life," she says.

***

After Linnea married Richard Rhodes, an Exxon chemical engineer, the couple moved to Elizabeth and then to Westfield. Raising her two sons, Rich and William, became a much different experience from the way she was reared by her working parents.

"I was home and very involved with the boys' schools," says the veteran PTA/PTO volunteer.

The independent ways of Linnea's generation in Maplewood were absent in the Westfield youngsters in the 70s and 1980s. Activities were more formalized, be it in sports or after-school classes.

"We were at every activity our kids did," says Linnea. "It was like spectator sports for parents. And many of these activities had professional teachers."

The days of hanging around the neighborhood after school were passé, for the most part.

"I swear I drove my kids two blocks to see a friend," recalls Linnea. "Why? I don't know."

Linnea expended much time helping her offspring with their homework, to the extent that it became a joke with her friends. At Linnea's 40th birthday party, Patty Noerr and a few others performed parodies of well-known songs---all about Linnea's homework-related mothering.

Today, Linnea looks back and admits: "I was way too involved with my kids."

In fact, in talks to parents of daycare clients, Linnea often spoke about her child-raising experiences and advised the attendees not to get over-involved in their children's lives.

***

She is proud, though, that her sons---now both in their 30s---are artists. William, the younger son, is a sculptor whose works have been exhibited in the New York area. Rich, who minored in painting, brought along canvases and brushes when the family took its annual vacation in New Hampshire in 1999. He joined his mother on a golf course as they painted the landscape.

"It was my first painting en plein air," says Linnea. "It's pitiful."

But it hangs for all to see at the vacation home the family owns in Stephenstown, N.Y.

Actually, since her retirement, Linnea spends up to six hours a day, three to four days a week in the winter months, in her new artistic interest: painting with oils and watercolors.

Her son William, who majored in art, often will look at the works and suggest she try it "this way" or another way. Most of Linnea's paintings are scenes from photos she has taken in her extensive travels. She promised her friends that someday these works would be displayed and sold at art shows. In early 2006, Linnea joined other local artists for a show and sold many of her paintings; among the buyers were a number of her Club '43 colleagues.

***

Life at 60-plus represents a much different world for Linnea than it did for her mother.

"My mother, who had been slender when she was young, was heavy and sedentary at this age. Today, I am active and more aware of heath concerns."

Linnea keeps in shape by eating sensibly, biking, and keeping active on the links.

"It spoke to me," she says about golf, which has been a passion of hers for about 15 years, starting with winter golf lessons---given in a gymnasium---at the town's Adult School.

Traveling also is a priority these days for Linnea.

"When I was young, we always went on vacation to the same place---Martha's Vineyard---or to camp or to visit people. I remember we would get up when it was still dark and start driving. My mother packed a lunch and we stopped to have picnics. And all I wanted to do was go to a restaurant."

Today, she and Richard get to dine at restaurants on the trips they take to Europe or Nova Scotia or ski areas out West. A visitor to the Rhodes home will see many of these places immortalized in the paintings that Linnea has created from her photos of those trips.

***

"They never run."

Ask Linnea Rhodes, the ex-daycare center director, what she thinks now about daycare in general, and you may be surprised by responses such as the aforementioned quote.

While working at Westfield Day Care Center ranks high on her list of lifetime memories and accomplishments, she sees some downsides to daycare in general.

She stresses that, unlike a generation ago when extended families were around and could help with babysitting chores, the modern daycare facilities provide needed services for parents who must work. Linnea believes, though, that a lot of mothers in towns like Westfield could stay home but thus would not be able to enjoy the lifestyle they seek. So they work and place their offspring in all-day care. She respects their decisions but personally thinks children would do better in their homes if they could remain there.

What is really a "shame," in her mind, though, is that children often spend eight to 10 hours in daycare. Their activity is controlled because of safety concerns and potential legal problems. As a result, she says, "they never run. They walk. They can't be kids. And often, when their parents pick them up, they are driven to another controlled activity."

That, she says, "is the sad part of daycare."

Linnea Rhodes

With brother (1945)
Skiing at Snowmass with sons (1976)
Brownie (1949)
With husband in Tuscany (1999)

Cathy Farrell Rock

June 17, 1961.

The U. S. Women's Open was in full swing at Baltusrol Golf Club in Springfield. N.J. The club's pro, Johnny Farrell, and his wife, Catherine, were busy working with the volunteers and competitors at the championship event.

Blocks away, their 17-year-old daughter, Cathy, sat on the steps outside her family's apartment near Hillside Avenue. She was waiting to be picked up by a high school friend and that girl's parents to drive to Michigan.

"I remember my friend was late; I think her father got mixed up between Hillside (a town) and Hillside Avenue," said Cathy.

Soon they arrived and off the young women went; on the way, they stopped at Notre Dame University in South Bend, Ind.

"We thought we'd see boys," says a smiling Cathy as she looks back at the day 40 years ago. "I can't believe that."

After all, she was heading for a new life.

As a nun.

***

Cathy Farrell Rock grew up in Westfield's prestigious Stoneleigh Park section as the youngest of five children. After the older ones had left home, Cathy and her parents moved to Springfield to the apartment near Baltusrol, a famous golf club whose members were mostly from blueblood WASP families.

At Balustrol, Johnny Farrell continued to build on the strong professional reputation he had made over the years. His most prized accomplishment came in 1928 at Olympia Fields in Illinois, where he beat the legendary Bobby Jones to win the U.S. Open. Seventy-five years later, in 2003, the Open returned to Olympia Fields and Cathy Rock joined the throngs in attendance. Cathy's brother, Bill Farrell, a golf pro, was on the green to represent the family as the trophy was awarded to Jim Furyk. The sponsoring United States Golf Association printed the Open tickets with vintage photos from the 1928 event.

"It was magical walking around and seeing everyone having a photo of Dad around their necks on the tickets," says Cathy, who called it "special" to sit near the green and relive what it must have been like for her father 75 years before.

Like others in the family, Cathy learned to play a mean round on the golf links. In fact, one day in 1966, Cathy, then Sister Mary Campion, joined her father for a few holes at Baltusrol. People on the clubhouse balcony were stunned to see a nun, in full habit with a 15-decade rosary swinging from her side, hitting a long shot to the green.

***

Cathy Farell spent her final two years of high school at Rosarian Academy in West Palm Beach, Fla. She had transferred from Benedictine Academy in Elizabeth, N.J., to be nearer her parents during the winter months when her father worked out of The Country Club of Florida.

"It was like a military school," she says about Rosarian, an all-girls' boarding school.

The nuns, members of the Dominican Order whose motherhouse was in Adrian, Mich., would flip quarters on the beds to see if the bedding was "taut enough," Cathy recalls. One day, she was sent back to the dorm from her classroom because her sink had water marks in it and that was considered unacceptable. Lights-out were at 8 or 8:30 p.m., with "Great Silence" imposed until the next morning.

In the dining room, a nun sat in the corner to ensure that the students ate everything on their plate. Cathy was amazed when they were served hot dogs split in half.

"I was new there and I said to the others: "why don't we get the hot dog in one piece?""

Her schoolmates looked at her as if to say the nuns think the girls might use it for other purposes, like pleasing themselves.

"With a hot dog?" responded Cathy. "Is this for real?

***

Cathy was among three of the 30 members of Rosarian's Class of 1961 to enter the order of the nuns who operated the school. Unlike other Dominican orders that might be affiliated with a diocese, the Adrian-based group is a Pontifical unit, thus under the direction of the Pope in Rome. At the time Cathy entered in 1961, the order had 2500 members.

Cathy was one of 97 young women to arrive in June; by the time they became novices six months later, the entering class was down to 75. As a novice, Cathy remained at the motherhouse and was given what she calls "prestigious" assignments, including caring for the Sacristy, the room where vestments and chalices are kept, and where the priests "vest" for Mass.

"I think I got the good assignments because of who my father was," said Cathy, happy not to have been assigned to more janitor-like tasks as were some of her fellow novices.

She also became a seamstress, since the nuns had to make everything they wore.

The rules at the motherhouse were "very monastic," according to Cathy, but basically not much different from the rules imposed at Rosarian Academy.

In January 1963, when she was 19, Cathy left Michigan to teach at the order's St. Mary of Mt. Carmel School in Chicago. It was the same year she would make her "first profession" in the convent and take the religious name, Sister Mary Campion.

Her mentor at St. Mary's was Sister Patrick Joseph Kelly, a survivor of the Titanic sinking in 1912. She and the other nuns "loved" Cathy's father, who visited when he could.

In those days, it was acceptable for nuns to start teaching at Catholic schools even before they completed their college education. It took Cathy seven years of summer school and part-time studies to complete her undergraduate degree in Latin and the classics at the order's Siena Heights College in Adrian, Mich.

In the 60s, Chicago was the city of Mayor Richard Daley and host to the riot- rocked Democratic National Convention in 1968. The Windy City was "so Catholic," Cathy says, that no one asked what part of the city you were from.

"It was always: 'what parish do you live in?'"

***

As Sister Mary Campion, Cathy could not go out after dark. She did not have a Social Security number----everything was provided for her. She never carried money---"we didn't need it," she says. She was unable to travel home for a few years after she entered the convent, so she missed such events as her sister's wedding in 1964.

On a home visit in 1965 to New Jersey, Cathy, per the rules of the order, brought along another nun as a traveling companion. They could not stay with Cathy's family, but rather were hosted at a nearby convent. The Sisters there were from another order with more liberal rules. At the time, the World's Fair was attracting thousands of people to Flushing, N.Y., about 30 miles from Springfield. Mr. Farrell told his daughter that they would be going to the Fair and that they would not be back until after dark---"no matter what those rules are." The nuns at the host convent had no idea about the Dominican rules so off went Sister Mary Campion---out at night for the first time in years!

***

In 1967, the year she took her final vows as a nun, Cathy was selected to be in a documentary titled "Inquiring Nuns." Her role was easy: she and another nun, microphones in hand, were bused to varied sections of Chicago to ask people one question: Are you happy? Almost across the board, the answers were linked to the individuals' feelings about the Vietnam War, then in full swing in Southeast Asia.

About three decades later, Cathy found out from a friend that "Inquiring Nuns" had made a list of top Catholic films recommended for viewing. Through a local video store in Westfield, she secured the film and showed it to her three children, then of college age or a bit older.

"They were hysterical," she laughs. "Here I was in the film in my early 20s in this nun's habit and all you could see was my face and I am asking people 'Are you happy?'"

***

When Cathy took her final vows in December 1967, her entering class was down to 55 from the original 97.

Things were changing in America and the world during the period, and the Catholic Church was no exception. The Vatican II Council in 1962 had initiated a series of changes, beginning with placement of the altar in churches so that priest could face those in the congregation. Orders of nuns became more worldly, with sisters starting to drive cars and becoming more involved in the community. Many nuns began wearing less formal clothing, more in line with traditional women's suits. And, in some cases, the nuns' religious names went by the wayside in favor of their given names. Thus, in 1968, Sister Mary Campion became Sister Catherine Farrell.

It also was the year she decided to leave the convent.

Cathy told her parents that she would be leaving the Dominican order, but had agreed to stay until the end of the school year the following June. She was 25, going on 26, and thought she was "old;" most of her friends from high school were married already. Cathy wondered if she would find someone to wed, and figured that she probably had a better chance of meeting someone her type while she was in the convent rather than waiting until her departure when, she figured, "my mother would want to use her matchmaking skills."

In March 1969, another St. Mary's teacher, a lay member of the faculty, said she and her fiancé were going out to dinner with a friend who had recently left the priesthood. She invited Cathy to join them.

Sister Catherine Farrell knew she would be exiting the order in a few months, but her wardrobe was still that of a nun. So she borrowed clothes from the friend. That night, she met Dave Rock, the ex-priest who had come from Rockford, Ill., for a job interview.

"I just met the man I am going to marry," she said as he walked toward her.

***

Cathy left the convent in June of that year.

"The years I was a nun---1961 to 1969---they are lost to me with reality," says Cathy. "I missed that era. The Vietnam years... I was the age of protestors but I could not protest as a nun. I never heard of the Beatles until 1969."

That fall, just a few months after Cathy shed her religious name, she and Dave were married. The Rocks lived in Wisconsin, where Cathy took a teaching job at a public school. Dave's background in canon law did not prepare him fully for a career outside the priesthood, so he earned a doctorate in educational administration at the University of Wisconsin, where Cathy also studied and completed her master's degree.

Her eight-year hiatus from golf did not hamper her play. In the early 1970s, she won the women's championship at Monroe Country Club, as well as the county championship and the Wisconsin state championship in her division.

***

In 1977, with their three preschoolers---Patrick, Eileen and Molly--- in tow, the Rocks moved to Westfield, Cathy's hometown, where Dave was hired as an assistant superintendent with the town school system. Six years later, Cathy returned to the classroom as an elementary school teacher in nearby Summit. Her goal was to move into administration and she began studying at Rutgers University for a doctorate in that field. She was hired in 1989 as principal of an elementary school in Watchung, N.J.

"At the time there were not a lot of women working as elementary school principals," said Cathy, who received her doctorate few years after assuming the principalship.

Cathy won the admiration of parents, students, and school board members in Watchung, so when an opening for superintendent came up in 1998, she was the overwhelming choice.

The work was "fulfilling," she says, as she describes the many facets of a superintendent's life and her pride at having led the move for the borough to pass a bond referendum to allow growth of the schools.

To what does she attribute the leadership she exhibited in that post and her work as president of the county chapter of the state's Association of School Administrators, as an adjunct professor at Rutgers, and a longtime church volunteer?

"I had good training," she states. "My mother was confident and strong; she was very active in the American Women's Volunteer Services. And my convent training was excellent. I also think going to all-girls high schools helped."

***

Cathy admits that her life does not mirror that of her mother, a model married at age 20.

"She never would have thought about a career. She was more high society."

But the connection to her mother is exemplified in such instances as when Cathy was the proud mother of the bridegroom at Patrick's wedding in 2003.

"I was 60 and I wore the dress my mother wore at age 60 to the White House when she and Daddy were invited to a state dinner that President Nixon had for the Duke of Windsor, who took golf lessons from my father. And the dress fit perfectly."

After seven years as superintendent, Dr. Catherine Rock stepped down in 2005 and she and her husband moved to a beautiful home in Florida. In her retirement, she will get "two new knees" to thwart an arthritis problem and also enjoy her children and grandchildren.

And, she promises, "I plan to go back to a single-digit handicap on the golf course."

Cathy Rock

Sister Mary Campion (1966)
In her mother's dress at
 son's wedding (2003)
Receiving doctorate (1995)

Madeleine
Walsh Sullivan

The assassination of President John F. Kennedy in 1963 shocked the nation to its core. Anyone of age at the time remembers exactly where he/she was that fateful day---Nov. 22, when the news broke across the world.

The infamous Friday proved sad for another reason for Madeleine Walsh Sullivan, then 20 years old and a junior at St. Mary of the Woods College near Terre Haute, Ind.

"I remember it so well," she says. "It was in the morning and I was studying in a dorm study hall for an American history test. Sister Marie Agatha, who was about six-foot-three---a young nun---came to the study hall and motioned me out. I thought I was in trouble for something."

Madeleine stood in the hall as the nun delivered shocking news: Madeleine's father, Thomas Joseph Walsh, 53, had died unexpectedly earlier that day in their hometown of Elizabeth, N.J.

The nun accompanied Madeline to her dorm room, where the latter's two roommates, who had been informed of the death, had packed their friend's clothes for the trip home.

Madeleine, the oldest of six children, had no money for the expensive trip east, but that proved no problem as the nuns had made arrangements.

"They drove me to the airport and I was put on a private plane to Indianapolis---I never knew how they got that."

Then Madeleine flew by commercial carrier to Idlewild, the airport that a month later would be renamed JFK International in honor of the slain president. When Madeleine alighted from the plane, she saw television sets covering the news about the assassination of the president.

The moment was almost surreal for Madeleine.

"Between my father and JFK, I thought the world must be ending."

***

For the next few days, people flocked to the wake in Elizabeth.

"Everyone who came talked about dad and JFK," says Madeleine. "My brother Tommy was angry---he wanted them to talk about dad---period."

Madeleine remembers other moments over the next few days: watching TV as Jack Ruby shot JFK's alleged killer, Lee Harvey Oswald; receiving cards "from just about everyone" at her college, and learning something she never knew about her father.

"When I was home, my Uncle Jack told us that my father had been married before he married my mother."

The first wife, Deborah VonBishophousen, had died from tuberculosis. Madeleine recalls that "my father's ex-father-in-law used to visit our home and my mother didn't like it. Now I knew why!'"

Almost two decades before, Madeleine's father had returned from his World War II service in Europe as a highly decorated captain. His wish, as expressed often by Madeleine's mother, Genevieve, and many of his friends, was to be buried at Arlington Cemetery in Virginia. But the death of JFK halted that dream---the late president was buried with worldwide news coverage the same day as the Walsh funeral in New Jersey.

Madeleine says her mother often would say that "had JFK not died, your father would have been buried in Arlington."

Instead, after a funeral mass attended by hundreds, Thomas Joseph Walsh was laid to rest at the Veterans Cemetery of New Jersey in Burlington.

Madeleine returned a week later to St. Mary of the Woods and almost immediately was asked to go to the motherhouse to meet Sister Mary Josephine, the head of the order. The nun handed Madeleine a check to cover her expenses for the rest of the year.

Those kindnesses have made an appreciative Madeleine a devoted alumna: "When they ask for money, I contribute."

***

Madeleine Walsh was born in October 1943 at Fort Benning, Ga., where her father was at Officer Candidates' School in preparation for his overseas assignment.

Her mother, Genevieve Boyle Walsh, reportedly almost died during the difficult birth; doctors recommended that she should have no more children.

"I always thought my mother was mad at the (Catholic) church because of no birth control rules," says Madeleine. "Every time she was pregnant, she was scared she would die."

Madeleine and her five siblings grew up in Elizabeth when it was considered one of the nicest cities in the Garden State. While her mother was a homemaker, her father had a series of sales jobs before becoming director of the Buildings Department at City Hall and then Elizabeth's Civil Defense director.

"I think he was depressed," says Madeleine about her dad, a Columbia University alumnus who smoked a lot of Chesterfields. "He was not really successful but didn't seem to know why. He had a lot of pressure with six kids."

Mr. Walsh wanted to make sure, though, that his children attended college. His plan: one would go to a good college and then the others would go with the help of those who had finished. His choice for his first offspring, Madeleine, was Manhattanville, a college that attracted many women from upper-middle class Catholic families. But Madeleine opted for St. Mary of the Woods after completing high school studies at Benedictine Academy in Elizabeth.

After her spouse's death, Genevieve faced the prospect of raising six children alone. She owed money to the Veterans Administration--her husband had borrowed it for a failed venture.

"My mother got it straightened out---she did not have to pay it," says Madeleine.

Two weeks after the funeral, Genevieve went to work in real estate at a firm owned by her family.

"She was good at it," says a proud Madeleine about her mother.

Being at college 800 miles from home, Madeleine usually returned to Elizabeth only at Christmas break. During her senior year---December 1964---she used her holiday vacation to look for jobs she might take after she received her liberal arts degree the following spring. She accepted a position with Barnes and Noble, then a small operation with one store at 19th Street and Fifth Avenue in Manhattan. Initially, Madeleine typed for a vice president, and within a month asked for a raise and more responsibility. Her duties included deciding about copyrights and working with rates and permissions. At night, she attended a Union Square school to study shorthand. And, just like most of her Club '43 classmates who entered the work world about the same time, she trekked to her job in often uncomfortable high heels.

Like many young women of the time, she lived at home. Madeleine paid room and board, a good way to ease the family financial burden after her father's passing.

But the New York job failed to intrigue Madeleine, so after a few months she left. She eventually took a job with Elizabeth's Welfare Board as its youngest caseworker. The $5,000 position came with a car, but Madeleine lacked a driver's license.

"So I got it," laughs Madeleine, who later was promoted to supervisor; in that role, she "handled lots of money."

It was the time of the escalation of the Vietnam War, and that conflict hit home in Elizabeth. Dickie Reilly, whose family lived next door to the Walsh family, asked Madeleine to marry him before he headed to the war zone.

"I think maybe he asked a lot of people," says Madeleine.

Reilly never returned; the boy-next-door died in Vietnam.

***

Madeleine continued to work after her marriage to Bill Sullivan, a Jersey City native whom she met in a bar---the standard matchmaking center of the 60s---but left her job prior to the birth of the Sullivans' first child, Brigitte. At the time, Madeleine's income surpassed that of her spouse, and job rules mandated that she leave when she was six months pregnant. Madeleine says she "lied about how pregnant I was" and stayed until almost a month before the birth. After Brigitte was born, Madeleine discovered that the Welfare Board had canceled her pension because her superiors figured she would not be returning. When she informed them she indeed planned to go back, she was told "you have four weeks off." The doctor would not release her for six weeks, so Madeleine resigned.

Six months later, Madeleine took a part-time job as Director of Welfare in North Plainfield, N.J. When she became pregnant with Maggie, her second daughter, Madeleine was forced to leave that post.

"They told me: 'we are going to hire someone else.'"

She shakes her head today as she mulls these job-related experiences and concludes "it's a lot different now!"

Madeleine's work career continued---she remained in social work before joining the Middletown, N.J., School District child study team years ago--- as did her dedication to further education. In 2002---not long before Club '43 would begin its year-long celebration to mark members' 60th birthdays---Madeleine was awarded her doctor of letters degree from Drew University. She thus joined the ranks of the other doctoral late-bloomers in Club '43---Tina Lesher and Cathy Rock earned their doctorates when they were in their 40s.

***

Life for Madeleine, Bill and their young daughters proved to be one of upper crust living. Bill's career escalated; he moved up the ranks at ADP to become head of one of its largest divisions. The Sullivan family employed a fulltime nanny/housekeeper and resided in a well-appointed home in Westfield's beautiful Indian Forest section; they also owned a summer home in Avon-by-the-Sea at the Jersey shore. By all measures, the family was enjoying a life that would make many jealous.

That is, until Madeleine reached age 42.

The number still resonates in her head.

"My mother was 42 when she was widowed; when I was 42, Bill left me."

She began to think of other similarities in the context of family.

"My grandfather (maternal) was named Bill, too. And like my husband, he was generous with his money and bought lots of gifts."

Bill Boyle, her grandfather, had donated a city block in Elizabeth and construction monies for the building of St. Genevieve's Church on the site. To this day, the family---now scattered in other New Jersey towns--- holds its weddings or funerals at the church.

In 1936, though, Boyle left Madeleine's grandmother, from whom he remained permanently separated.

***

After her divorce, Madeline felt inept and unattractive. Facing what she calls "The Dating Game" seemed frightening to her.

She remembered when her widowed mother moved into the dating realm.

Once, when Madeleine was in her early 20s, a man came to pick up her mother for a date.

"She did not want the guy to think she had children that old, so I became her sister that day!"

A colleague encouraged Madeleine to attend a weekly singles' event in Morristown; a typical evening included small-group discussions followed by a dance.

"I couldn't believe someone asked me to dance; he said he had six kids and I laughed."

One time there she met a former Jesuit priest whom she began to date. He read her poetry in Latin and she loved it.

But her daughters did not like him---or some others their mother dated.

"It was awful," says Madeleine.

One outlet for her was a return to school. Already armed with a MA in student personnel services, she headed to Fordham for her MSW, which she earned in 1992. Both of her daughters also hold that degree from Fordham; as an alumna, Madeleine presented them their degrees at Avery Fisher Hall, Lincoln Center.

"That was thrilling to me," states Madeleine. "Having daughters with the same degree also gives us an opportunity to share something in common."

School---and being successful at it---made Madeleine "more confident." She followed her Fordham studies with a three-year program in family therapy at the Multicultural Family Institute and opened a part-time therapy practice.

When she could, Madeleine traveled to interesting places, including Japan, Hong Kong, Yugoslavia, and Italy; she says traveling by herself proved to be a "great adventure."

***

A few years ago, while she was on sabbatical in Ireland to do research for her doctoral dissertation, Madeleine began dating Donal Hackett, a tall, handsome Irishman who is 15 years her junior. He has visited Westfield on several occasions and has walked Madeleine up the aisle at her daughters' weddings.

Although Madeleine, now a grandmother, believes it is still hard to be divorced in society, she feels she has weathered the storm and proclaims marriage need not be in the offing.

"I can do it myself," says Madeleine proudly.

After all, she notes, her mother became a successful career woman and was dating in her 60s.

Then she adds: "Of course, she remarried at age 66."

Madeleine Sullivan

At daughter's wedding (2006)
Bride (1970)
Receiving doctorate (2003)

Judi Shaubach Thompson

Life in Lancaster County in Pennsylvania offered a "sheltered" upbringing for Judi Shaubach Thompson. Diversity was a non-issue.

"There were no blacks in my high school class. Even at Penn State, there weren't that many."

In her mid-thirties, though, Judi took a position with the Elizabeth, N.J. schools, with a diverse population in an urban setting.

After five years as a business education teacher, she moved to a faculty position with the district's Pregnant Teens Program.

About 80 pregnant students were enrolled in the Elizabeth program every year---that was the same number in the entire class at Lampeter-Strasburg High School in Pennsylvania, where Judi was graduated in 1960.

"At LSHS, a couple both had to quit school and take the GED (Graduate Equivalency Diploma) test to finish," says Judi. "The girl was pregnant and they got married, but they still had to quit. In the 14 years I worked in the Elizabeth program, maybe five students got married in all."

The average age of the Elizabeth pregnant teens was 16, and most were not "overachievers," according to Judi. "Once in a while, we even had middle school kids in the program."

Yet she found her work with the Pregnant Teens Program to be "incredibly fulfilling.

"We took care of them," states Judi. "We were their advocates."

In addition to instruction in English, history and business, the program provided guidance counselors, and social workers. A nurse came regularly to check on the girls.

The scenario represented a complete about-turn from the way young women were treated back at her Pennsylvania high school 20 years before. When Judi was a high school senior, a few freshmen girls got pregnant. They had to leave school, she recalls, because they were considered "loose." That attitude was considered the norm for American schools at the time.

***

Growing up in Strasburg, Judi says, meant locking the house and putting the key under the door mat. Youngsters walked to grammar school everyday, and came home for lunch.

"It was safe and idyllic. You were never afraid," states Judi, about the heavily Republican town.

In the late 50s, she would read about then-President Dwight "Ike" Eisenhower: "I thought all he did was play golf."

She "loved" going to visit the farms owned by both sets of her grandparents. For awhile, her paternal grandmother lived at the Shaubach home, but Judi says it was "not so good" a situation.

Her father, Park, worked in sales for Agway and her mother, Esther, took a part-time job at a department store when Judi, an only child, was in middle school. Esther later worked in secretarial posts and still, in her 80s, continues to work part-time. For more than 40 years, she has been a once-a-week Red Cross volunteer at Lancaster General Hospital.

As Judi got older, all she could think about was getting out of Strasburg.

"I remember sitting on the front porch and watching the cars go by on the main street. It was boring. I wanted to get out."

Her high school activities centered mainly in cheerleading and baton twirling. In addition to heading the school's majorette squad, Judi competed with a local group called the Pretzelettes, named for the teacher/coach who once won the local Pretzel Queen title in Lititz, the pretzel capital of the world. Judi proved to be a talented twirler, and had a solo act in a number of the performances.

"We didn't dress as pretzels, but we were quite sophisticated," says Judi, emphasizing that "we were not the sneaker-and-panty hose variety of today. We were traditional with boots and tassels."

Though she enrolled in college prep classes in high school, Judi envisioned moving onto the Katherine Gibbs Secretarial School and working in a senator's office. But her mother was adamant that Judi go to college and have the experiences that the former lacked.

"My mother really wanted me to have fun," says Judi. "And she never taught me to cook!"

***

So Judi chose the venerable and large Penn State, known as much for its football team as for its strong educational offerings. It took her a short time to realize that her so-called college prep courses were not comparable to those at other schools.

"We were not challenged in high school. I did not have the education my college friends had. I felt a bit unprepared."

She was also homesick because, she says, "I was emotionally attached to my mother." As a result, Judi almost dropped out of Penn State.

Then she joined a sorority, Alpha Omicron Phi, and things changed.

"I loved Penn State," she says. "It was wonderful."

She lived in the dorm because sororities, unlike the 50 fraternities on campus, did not have individual houses. The curfews were considered liberal at the time---11 p.m. on weekdays and 1 a.m. (sometimes 2 a.m.) on weekends. Unlike today, no boys were allowed in girls' rooms.

"Greek life was strong," Judi says, recalling "good times" she and her sorority sisters had at the "crazy fraternity parties---drinking green beer, and dancing the Twist and The Frug at jam sessions. When the IFC (Interfraternity Council) showed up, we'd hide the liquor."

After starting out in liberal studies, Judi majored in business education and had about a B average.

"I never wanted to push myself too much academically, so I figured this way I could teach or go to business. I wasn't excited about teaching, really, but I thought I'd have two options. And most women took education at the time."

As for Vietnam, she maintains she was "off the cusp of antiwar sentiment. I was not involved in protests."

During the summers she worked in Lancaster, close to Strasburg, just as the tourist business began to flourish around the Amish communities there. She worked in a coffee shop one summer, and as a chambermaid another year. The salaries allowed her to cover her spending money at school, and her parents paid for her education.

"I never went to the beach to work in the summer like some of my friends did," she says.

While she was in college, her parents got divorced. Judi says succinctly that "they were not a loving couple for many years."

She finished Penn State---the first in her family to receive a college degree---and applied for a teaching job in New Jersey because the salaries exceeded those in the Keystone State.

Judi taught business at Morristown High School for a few years, while sharing a third- floor apartment.

"But I got sick of bells and the whole routine of schools---I wanted something different," she says.

So, in 1968, she headed for New York and Wall Street, where she worked at a few small investment banks, eventually taking charge of bookkeeping, payroll and personnel at one of these firms. She first lived with a friend of a friend on the upper East Side and later moved down to the East 33rd Street. She met her future husband---Richard Thompson---in Bay Head, the Jersey shore town that was a mecca for single professionals on summer weekends.

***

For her wedding in 1971, Judi eschewed the traditional church reception that was typical of post-marriage ceremonies at her Strasburg church and had the reception at a Sheraton in the area.

"We had a champagne toast. That was it. No liquor! Frankly, I let my mother have too much say about it."

The Thompsons moved to Elizabeth, N.J. and then to nearby Cranford, and Judi became a commuter to her Manhattan job. In 1976, she gave birth to the couple's only child, a son named Chad. A year-and-a-half later, Judi decided she wanted to return to the working world, but no longer sought a long commute to Wall Street. She chose to return to teaching and, in 1977, joined the faculty at Elizabeth High as a business education teacher.

"What a difference from Morristown, where the students were more sophisticated than I was," she says. "Elizabeth was totally urban."

She hired a capable woman to care for Chad and "never had a problem about what could happen. It was easier then," she says.

She was transferred to the Board of Education Building to work with the Pregnant Teens Program, but the program was disbanded in the mid-1990s. So Judi found herself back at Elizabeth High as a business education teacher. The specialty had changed in the intervening years. Typing class had given way to Introduction to Computer Applications and computer science.

"I was nervous," Judi says, "because I hadn't kept up with technology. Even though I was skeptical and apprehensive, it all worked out fine."

***

When Judi was 42, she was diagnosed with breast cancer. Her son was 8 at the time.

"I was petrified I wouldn't be around to see him grow up," she remarks.

A month after the lump was discovered, Judi underwent a mastectomy. Although she did not need chemotherapy or radiation, she did have reconstructive surgery.

The caring attitude of coworkers and students at the Pregnant Teens Program was exemplified, she says, as she fought the disease.

"Everyone there was so supportive," says Judi, who missed six weeks of work.

When Judi was discharged after a week at Columbia Presbyterian Hospital in Manhattan, her mother came to help.

"Why couldn't it be me?" implored Esther Shaubach, then 63, to her daughter.

Five years later, after the Thompson family had moved to a home in Westfield, Judi's breast cancer appeared again.

"I was devastated the first time," she says. "It was a shock to me the second time. I felt my body had betrayed me."

Doctors had discovered suspicious lesions in scar tissue. Judi had radiation treatments at Overlook Hospital, a few miles from her home, and took tamoxifen pills that reportedly interfere with estrogen activity. Most of her treatments took place in the summer when Judi was on break from her teaching duties. Again, her friends and family provided strong support.

"I have had no problem since then," she says. "I feel fine. I got to the point where I just don't worry about this. I figure I probably will be okay; if not, that's okay. It's out of my control."

She marvels, though, at the insensitivities exhibited by some people when it comes to breast cancer.

"A man once said to me: 'I heard you had a slice job.' It was insensitive...unbelievable. I was speechless."

***

Now, at age 63, Judi Thompson has exited teaching and joined the world of the American retiree.

Her plans?

To do "something!"

"I am not going to sit. I don't want to clean out the basement. I am not artsy and craftsy. I want to make a contribution."

She definitely wants to add to her travel log---Judi already has been to Greece, other European countries, Alaska, etc.

Among her regular upcoming "trips" will be more 230-mile treks to State College, Pa., home of the Penn State Nittany Lions.

"I went to a lot of games there when I was a student," she smiles. "But I was 59 years old before I became a season ticket holder. My son had a lot to do with it. He is an avid sports fan."

And as she looks back at her life, Judi wonders what it would have been like had she never left Strasburg.

"Who is to say what would have been? I appreciate where I came from and where I am now."

Judi Thompson

Memorial Day Parade (1960)
Alaska Cruise with husband (2001)
With family (2004)

Loretta Ciraolo Wilson

Since her childhood days in Westfield, Loretta Ciraolo Wilson's personality has been marked by a sense of inquisitiveness.

This was evidenced when she was 6 years old and regularly passed a nearby Baptist church where most of the congregants were black.

The curious child "just had to see" where all the music was coming from, so she walked to the church entrance. A woman came out and invited Loretta in as the choir was singing "Hallelujah!"

"The woman gave me a tambourine," recalls Loretta, "and then she said: 'when I point to you, you hit it!' I loved it and got to hit the tambourine more than anybody else got to use their instruments."

Loretta's mother was not happy when she heard about her daughter's visit to the church.

"My mother was a very strict Catholic," says Loretta, "and when I asked her about going into any other church, she said our religion forbade us from going into other churches and I would be sent to hell. I never returned to the church because someone saw my bike there and informed my mother who reiterated that I had chosen the path of the devil and she did mourn about it for years."

***

Biagio Ciraolo, Loretta's father, was born in America in 1920. When he was 2, his mother died while giving birth to another son, so Biagio and his infant brother were sent to Sicily to be raised by an aunt and uncle.

"They had three children of their own," Loretta says, "and they would eat first, offering leftovers to the two boys."

Since that time, Loretta notes, her father has had a preoccupation with food; in his daily trips to Shop-Rite, he checks prices per pound and squeezes produce and fruit.

While his sons were in Sicily, Loretta's grandfather worked hard to make money to assist with their care and save for their return to the States. The boys were teenagers when they were reunited with their father.

Loretta's mother, the former Cornelia Monaco, came to Westfield from her native Italy when she was 9. Her father was a builder who constructed many of Westfield's colonial homes.

Biagio and Cornelia were married in 1942; their only child, Loretta, was born the next year.

Loretta's father had a series of jobs, with his longest stint at a girdle factory.

"He actually introduced some ideas they could use there," chuckles Loretta. "It all reminds me of a Seinfeld bit."

At one point, he opened a barber shop on Cumberland Street in Westfield and did well during the first year.

"Then the Beatles hit America, long hair became fashionable for men and his business died as the Four Tops retired and crew cuts became a thing of the past, "says Loretta. "So he closed up shop and took a job with a newly-opened convalescent center."

Biagio, now an octogenarian, continues to regale his family with scores of fascinating tales about his experiences in life. Loretta continually reminds her three sons to remember, when they see the famous tape of baseball great Lou Gehrig giving his farewell talk in 1939, that their grandfather was 19 then and in the stands at Yankee Stadium to witness the historic event.

Loretta's mother became a seamstress, joining her own mother in the 1930s at the pay-by-piece factory of the McGregor Co. in Summit, several miles north of Westfield.

A job at McGregor was not easy to secure.

"My mother started there as a kid," explains Loretta. "She was spoken for, meaning she had a mother and cousins already there. You had to know someone to get a job."

The dedicated seamstresses did not allow bad weather to hamper their workdays.

"When it snowed, my mother and grandmother would walk from Westfield, no kidding," says Loretta, about the difficult five-mile trek up and down hills. "Guess they were more accustomed to walking than we are!"

***

Day care, as it exists today, was not available in the 1940s in Westfield. At one point, Loretta's working mother put her daughter in the care of a woman who owned the home where the Ciraolos lived.

What was the punishment there if Loretta acted up?

"I was sent to the basement," she states.

Not wanting their daughter to go to her local southside public school---they felt it was not as good as those on Westfield's northside---Loretta's parents enrolled her when she was 4 at St. Christopher's School, located in a large home on a corner in downtown Mountainside. She was transported to school by her mother's car pool.

Loretta describes her St. Christopher's principal as a white-haired, bright woman who "would hit us. But, in those days, schools got no complaints from parents. My mother would just tell me to listen to the principal."

The principal, Loretta claims, "didn't allow us to talk about, look at and certainly not try writing script...she would hit us across the knuckles with a ruler if we did." The St. Christopher's School report cards included more than the typical grades.

"My report card once said I went to too many movies...that they were detrimental to me and stimulated me too much," says Loretta.

Still, the school provided intellectual experiences not offered in the public schools, including Latin instruction starting in second grade.

For lunch, students at St. Christopher's School always got a "big, hot meal," recalls Loretta. "And we always had potatoes and dessert."

The dessert, though, usually had the principal's hair in it," laughs Loretta. "She knew it and she made us eat it anyway."

To this day, Loretta is turned off to apple pie.

***

The Ciraolos worked hard to save their money, and in 1954 moved to a new house.

"They were able to custom-build their northside home on Salter Place," states Loretta. "It was built by family members---all in the trade."

Loretta then switched to public education at Westfield's Elm Street School.

She found herself behind only in writing script, but well-prepared by St. Christopher's in academic subjects.

Growing up---physically---proved difficult in some respects for Loretta. By her own description, she was bosomy for her age and embarrassed to the point that she would use her books to cover herself as she walked down the school stairs.

At Roosevelt Junior High School, teachers complained that Loretta was not using her brainpower. She had a high IQ but disliked doing homework.

"They said they wanted me to use my faculties," recalls Loretta about her teachers.

As a student, she felt that she was not encouraged to think outside the box.

"I did what I had to do to pass my courses."

One day, Loretta thought she had found a good way to boost her faltering science grade; as she was riding her Schwinn bike to Roosevelt, she saw a dead skunk on South Avenue and put it in a bag. She walked into her classroom and said: "Mr. Hart---look what I brought for extra credit."

The science teacher was not amused, and promptly hurled the smelly carcass out on the school's roof.

Loretta struggled a bit in her sewing class---an assignment to sew a Blackwatch jumper proved to be too difficult, especially because she deliberately had added to the length on the front and forgot to do that on the back. So she had to call on her seamstress-mother to assist with the final product

But Loretta did acquire some permanent sewing skills: "To this day, if I put a button on something, it will last forever."

***

She moved on to Westfield High School and, like many other teenagers of the period, found herself in trouble for smoking. The vice principal of discipline caught Loretta smoking and suspended her from school for three days. She was told that her father had to

call the vice principal's office and confirm that his daughter had told him about the suspension.

So, Loretta says, "I entreated several friends to call in and pretend to be my father, and all but one said no. However, the ones who said no forgot to tell me that they changed their minds and placed a call. So when I returned to school, I went into the vice principal's office and asked if he had heard from my father."

"Yes," he boomed. "I heard from all 10 of your fathers."

"We laughed like hell," says Loretta abut her conversation that day with the vice principal.

***

Prior to getting her driver's license, Loretta took a high school "Safe Driver" course. She was driving with the instructor one day when they came across a flock of birds in the road. Loretta slammed on the brakes to avoid hitting them. The instructor turned to her and yelled: "Don't ever stop for birds. They ALWAYS get out of the way."

She never forgot the lesson.

The athletic Loretta became captain of the WHS girls' basketball team and an active member of the Future Business Leaders of America.

While her academic achievements did not match her capabilities, Loretta says a "young Westfield High teacher worked with me, encouraging me to apply to colleges."

***

Loretta was only 16 when she completed high school. Her maternal grandparents had moved to Florida and Loretta decided to head south and attend the University of Miami at Coral Gables, where she lived on campus.

But one day Loretta was driving her grandparents' car; her grandmother and aunt were in the back seat. All of a sudden, while on a hilly road, they came upon a large group of birds beyond the next bend. Loretta did not alter her speed and her grandmother and aunt yelled in unison: "Watch out for the birds! You are going to kill them."

Loretta said: "Don't worry; they ALWAYS get out of the way."

call the vice principal's office and confirm that his daughter had told him about the suspension.

So, Loretta says, "I entreated several friends to call in and pretend to be my father, and all but one said no. However, the ones who said no forgot to tell me that they changed their minds and placed a call. So when I returned to school, I went into the vice principal's office and asked if he had heard from my father."

"Yes," he boomed. "I heard from all 10 of your fathers."

"We laughed like hell," says Loretta abut her conversation that day with the vice principal.

***

Prior to getting her driver's license, Loretta took a high school "Safe Driver" course. She was driving with the instructor one day when they came across a flock of birds in the road. Loretta slammed on the brakes to avoid hitting them. The instructor turned to her and yelled: "Don't ever stop for birds. They ALWAYS get out of the way."

She never forgot the lesson.

The athletic Loretta became captain of the WHS girls' basketball team and an active member of the Future Business Leaders of America.

While her academic achievements did not match her capabilities, Loretta says a "young Westfield High teacher worked with me, encouraging me to apply to colleges."

***

Loretta was only 16 when she completed high school. Her maternal grandparents had moved to Florida and Loretta decided to head south and attend the University of Miami at Coral Gables, where she lived on campus.

But one day Loretta was driving her grandparents' car; her grandmother and aunt were in the back seat. All of a sudden, while on a hilly road, they came upon a large group of birds beyond the next bend. Loretta did not alter her speed and her grandmother and aunt yelled in unison: "Watch out for the birds! You are going to kill them."

Loretta said: "Don't worry; they ALWAYS get out of the way."

After Loretta had plowed through the birds and it was obvious they had not survived, her grandmother and aunt cried and uttered such remarks as "How could you?"

Loretta answered: "My teacher lied to me."

Soon the trio had a fit of laughter, according to Loretta.

After two years at Miami, Loretta returned to New Jersey and continued her studies at Union College near Westfield.

***

Loretta's business career started with a job as a clerk and then a secretary at S& H Green Stamps in Metuchen, N.J. Soon she was promoted and transferred to the firm's home office in Manhattan. She climbed the ranks to assume a post as assistant to the vice president of consumer relations, an arm of the marketing division; she had 27 people reporting to her.

Through her association with American Women in Radio and Television, Loretta served on the planning committee for New York Gov. Nelson Rockefeller's Conference on the Status of Women. She later became involved in the first national commission with the consumer movement and attended a White House meeting of the Consumer Federation.

In early 1969, she married chemist Richard Wilson in a ceremony at Westfield's Holy Trinity Church. The pair met as fellow commuters. Loretta normally took the train from Westfield to Hoboken and continued by ferry to New York, but when the railroads went on strike, everyone took buses that became overcrowded quickly.

Richard got on the bus in Fanwood, and by the time it got to South Chestnut Street in Westfield and Loretta got on one day, the seats were filled. Richard offered her his seat and she refused, saying he got on first and thus should keep the seat.

He kept offering, and she kept refusing. "By the time we neared the (Newark) airport," says Loretta, "one of the other commuters said: 'Lady, please take his seat; I am trying to read my paper.'"

Richard kept pursuing Loretta at her office. When he would call her there, with the intent of asking her to go out on a date, Loretta had her secretaries on alert: "Tell him I am on the phone or in a meeting."

He kept trying until Loretta finally gave in.

"We met in July and were married in February," says Loretta, adding that she later learned that Richard had told his fellow commuter (who served as their best man) that he had noticed Loretta before the day they met on the bus and decided he was going to marry her.

Their wedding marked the first time that Holy Trinity Church allowed participation from a clergyman from another church. Determining what should be on the invitations was a problem, with the result being that Holy Trinity's Rev. John Murphy *officiated* and Rev. Dr. Clark Hunt (of Westfield's First Methodist Church) *participated.*

"It was such a big deal," remembers Loretta.

The Wilsons lived in Monmouth Beach and Edison before purchasing a home in Westfield in 1972. They have three sons: David, a Louisiana resident who is married and has two children; Donald and Jim.

One day, in 1971, Richard gave Loretta an ad that said "you can earn $20,000 a year in the real estate field." That propelled Loretta into a job at the Burke Agency in Scotch Plains, where she worked with seven men---and "learned so much" from them, especially how they viewed the real estate market.

Loretta challenged the agency's owner, Larry Burke, to give her more credit for the work she was doing. He told her that as long as she had a desk, her work was good.

"He went on vacation and I sold seven houses in a week," she laughs.

Loretta has worked for several local realty firms, and now is affiliated with Century 21---Taylor & Love in Westfield. She admits that her career often conflicted with motherhood and that "many times, I decided that my sons came first."

Things have changed in the real estate field, according to Loretta. When she started, men dominated the real estate sales force; now, many women work in that field.

Credit applications for home buyers once discouraged women from having children, she says.

"In 1971, mortgage lenders would only consider a woman's income toward a mortgage payment if she were a teacher or a nurse, and had been employed by one employer for some time. Even then, they would only count one-third of her income and some required a 'pill' note stating that the woman was on the birth control pill."

Her take on the changes relative to mortgage applications over the years?

"We've come a long way, baby!"

***

Like others in Club '43, the organization's "60 for "60" walk in 2003 remains a key memory for Loretta, one of the club's breast cancer survivors. Not only did she play an integral part in the planning for the event that raised monies for cancer research, but she brought along a special person to join in the festivities: her mother, Cornelia, who had supported Loretta when she faced the cancer bout eight years before. Cornelia Ciraolo died the following year.

***

Most Club '43 members know little about growing up and attending school in Westfield; they have viewed those things only through their roles as parents rearing their children in the town. Loretta, from her vantage point as one who has spent just about all of her life in Westfield, has emerged as an informal raconteur of sorts, one who over the years has provided verbal---and often humorous--- glimpses into life in Westfield over a generation.

She has witnessed the plummeting of what she calls "the pretentiousness" that once existed from some people in the upscale community.

"That has changed significantly," she states.

And asked how she would describe her lifetime in colonial Westfield, Loretta smiles and remarks: "Interesting. It has been interesting."

Loretta Wilson

With husband
(1995)
At 3 years old
(1946)
Bride (1968)
With family at
parents' 50th
Anniversary
(1991)

Conclusion

As a group, we Club '43 members have somewhat mirrored each other in our respective adult lives.

We all settled in a lovely New Jersey community. We focused our energy on providing the warm comforts of life for our families. We also assumed professional posts and enjoyed a high level of success in that regard.

As we participated in the fundraising "60 for 60" walk, we looked like a typical group of newly minted sexagenarians enjoying life at that age.

Unlike our mothers at age 60, though, most Club '43 members were not grandmothers as we entered our seventh decade (God forbid---seven decades!).

We remain active women whose lives extend from high-powered offices to gyms and golf courses. We have traveled extensively and some of us have lived overseas. As a group, we have a strong record of educational credits.

And while the trappings of suburbia may have made us fairly ordinary and similar in the context of Westfield living, each Club '43 member has an individual story to tell about her route to the 60-plus status.

***

One thing stands out among us, though, and that was expressed to me by Mary McEnenery after she read the manuscript for this book.

"We all had strong mothers, Tina," she said. "Imagine the influence that had on us."

In my youth in Pennsylvania, I knew few mothers who worked outside the home.

But the majority of mothers of Club '43 members had jobs---that statistic probably defies the norm for the 1950s and 1960s. Some of the other mothers, including my own, devoted endless hours to volunteer causes.

So it no doubt is true---our mothers' strength has become our legacy.

***

Through the profiles herein, a reader, especially one of the next generation, might understand how history has entered into the lives of Club '43 members. I have tried to start each individual chapter with an interesting anecdote/material that illuminates what it was like for us during varied periods of our lives; these illustrations are historical gems, in many cases.

The quotes from Club '43 members provide such fascinating detail to the overall work. Interviewing each of these women proved a joy for me.

Of course, writing about yours truly may have been the hardest part of the project; after all, I have a lifetime of information to extricate about myself. But I wanted to present the material in third-person format, much like profiles penned by a journalist. My newspaper/ academic background served me well in this endeavor.

So did the hard work of my friend, Linnea Rhodes, who, at my behest, assumed the informal title of "assistant editor." Not only did she offer to use her artistic talents to paint our group for the cover, but collected and handled all of the photos inserted herein.

In sum: I view this book as a way for people to understand how life changes over the decades---and as a way to honor a special group of friends.

Let me know if you, too, enjoyed reading about Club '43...

tinalesher@comcast.net

Printed in the United States
52972LVS00007B/1-234